WHY ARE THERE NO CATS IN THE BIBLE?

WHY ARE THERE NO CATS IN THE BIBLE?

AND OTHER FASCINATING FACTS TO EXPAND YOUR KNOWLEDGE OF THE BIBLE

George Davidson

CHARTWELL
BOOKS, INC.

Picture credits

26 Mary Evans; 189 Journeys of St. Paul, Map 2, © 2006,
Biblical Studies Press; reprinted with permission from
www.bible.org.; all other images Clipart

This edition printed in 2009 by

CHARTWELL BOOKS, INC.

A Division of **BOOK SALES, INC.**

276 Fifth Avenue Suite 206
New York, New York 10001 USA

ISBN-13: 978-0-7858-2493-0
ISBN-10: 0-7858-2493-6

Printed in China

CONTENTS

INTRODUCTION

This book is a miscellany of interesting information and fascinating facts. It is not a systematic commentary on the Bible, and it is certainly not a textbook of theology. It does not set out to provide a balanced summary of the whole Bible. The information it offers is sometimes serious, sometimes amusing, sometimes totally unexpected and off-the-wall, but it is never irreverent. This book is, after all, a companion to the Book of Books. Nothing I have written is intended to question or disparage the faith of any believer, but the Christian Church is a broad church, and there are differences of interpretation and opinion, which I have sometimes drawn attention to.

The version of the Bible which I have used for quotation is the King James or Authorized Version, the book that is for many Christians the definitive Word of God in English.

It has been said that the best way to learn about something is to write a book about it. That has been my experience. Even after a lifetime of religious studies, I was not surprised to find, as I wrote this book, some large gaps in my knowledge of the Bible. I owe the publishers a debt of gratitude for actually paying me for four months of intensive Bible study. They got a book:

I got so much more.

Finally, I would like to thank Martin Manser, Dr Debra Reid and the Rev. John Davidson for their many helpful comments and suggestions.

George Davidson

THE BIBLE: THE BOOK OF BOOKS
... AND A BOOK OF BOOKS

The Bible is not one book but a collection of books. It was originally written on separate scrolls containing one or more of the books. It has been calculated that the Bible was written over a period of more than 1,400 years by at least 40 different people.

The word 'Bible' is derived through Latin from the Greek phrase *ta biblia*, meaning 'the books'. In Latin, *biblia* came to be understood as a singular noun meaning 'the book'. Greek *biblia* is derived from *biblos* 'papyrus', from Byblos, the name of a Phoenician port (now Jubayl in Lebanon) from which papyrus was exported to Greece.

The first use of *ta biblia* meaning 'the Bible' is in a Christian document known as *2 Clement*, which contains a sermon written about the middle of the 2nd century AD.

The Bible consists of two parts, the Old Testament and the New Testament. The Christian Old Testament is also the Jewish Bible (although there are a few differences). The New Testament is the second part of the Christian Bible.

The word 'testament' in the biblical sense means 'covenant'. The Old Testament records several covenants made between God and mankind, such as the covenant with Noah after the Flood (Genesis 9:8–17), the covenant with Abraham (Genesis 15 and 17) promising that his descendants will possess Canaan, and in particular the covenant made with Moses and the Israelites at Sinai (Exodus 19–24) after they had escaped from Egypt. The New Testament records the new covenant between God and mankind, instituted by Jesus at the Last Supper before his trial and crucifixion:

This is my blood of the new testament, which is shed for many. (Mark 14:24)

The apostle Paul also speaks of this 'new testament' (2 Corinthians 3:6).

THE BOOKS OF THE BIBLE

Old Testament (39 books)					
Book	**Chapters**	**Book**	**Chapters**	**Book**	**Chapters**
Genesis	50	2 Chronicles	36	Danie	12
Exodus	40	Ezra	10	Hosea	14
Leviticus	27	Nehemiah	13	Joel	3
Numbers	36	Esther	10	Amos	9
Deuteronomy	34	Job	42	Obadiah	1
Joshua	24	Psalms	150	Jonah	4
Judges	21	Proverbs	31	Micah	7
Ruth	4	Ecclesiastes	1	Nahum	3
1 Samuel	31	Song of Solomon	8	Habakkuk	3
2 Samuel	24	Isaiah	66	Zephaniah	3
1 Kings	22	Jeremiah	52	Haggai	2
2 Kings	25	Lamentations	5	Zechariah	14
1 Chronicles	29	Ezekiel	48	Malachi	4

New Testament (27 books)					
Book	**Chapters**	**Book**	**Chapters**	**Book**	**Chapters**
Matthew	28	Ephesians	6	Hebrews	13
Mark	16	Philippians	4	James	5
Luke	24	Colossians	4	1 Peter	5
John	21	1 Thessalonians	5	2 Peter	3
Acts	28	2 Thessalonians	3	1 John	5
Romans	16	1 Timothy	6	2 John	1
1 Corinthians	16	2 Timothy	4	3 John	1
2 Corinthians	13	Titus	3	Jude	1
Galatians	6	Philemon	1	Revelation	22

SOME BIBLE FACTS AND FIGURES

English translations of the Bible generally contain over 750,00 words and around 3.5 million letters. The following figures apply to the Authorized or King James Version of the Bible:

	Old Testament	New Testament	Bible
Number of books in the …	39	27	66
Number of chapters in the …	929	260	1,189
Number of verses in the …	23,214	7,959	31,173
Number of words in the …	593,493	181,253	774,746
Number of letters in the …	2,728,100	838,380	3,566,480

By comparison, the Old Testament in Hebrew contains 308,428 words.

◆ *The middle book of the Old Testament is Proverbs; the middle chapter is Job 29 and the middle verses are 2 Chronicles 20:17–18.*

◆ *The middle book of the New Testament is 2 Thessalonians; the middle chapters are Romans 13 and 14; and the middle verse is Acts 17:17.*

◆ *The middle books of the Bible are Micah and Nahum; and the middle chapter is Psalm 117.*

◆ *By the number of words, the shortest book in the Bible is the Third Letter of John; by the number of verses, the Second Letter of John. The shortest book in the Old Testament is Obadiah.*

◆ *The longest book in the Bible is Psalms; Luke wrote the two longest books of the New Testament (Luke's Gospel and Acts).*

◆ *The shortest chapter in the Bible is Psalm 117 (2 verses) and the longest is Psalm 119*

(176 verses). The longest chapter in the New Testament is Luke 1 (80 verses).

◆ The shortest verse in the Old Testament is 1 Chronicles 1:25: 'Eber, Peleg, Reu'. It occurs in a long list of names. 1 Chronicles 1:1, 1:2, 1:3, 1:24 and 1:26 also consist of nothing more than three names each, but the names are longer.

◆ The shortest verse in the New Testament, and in the Bible, is John 11:35: two words – 'Jesus wept.' Another short verse is Luke 17:32: 'Remember Lot's wife.'

◆ The longest verse in the Bible is Esther 8:9 (90 words). The longest verse in the New Testament is Revelation 20:4 (67 words).

◆ 'Everlasting life' occurs 15 times in the Bible, but 'everlasting fire' only twice and 'everlasting punishment' once. The word 'eternity' occurs only once, in Isaiah 57:15.

◆ 'Girl' is used only twice in the Bible, at Joel 3:3 and Zechariah 8:5; 'boy' appears three times, at Genesis 25:27, and in Joel and Zechariah.

◆ Dogs are mentioned many times in the Bible, cats not even once. Cats are the only common domestic animal not mentioned in the Bible. (But see page 50.)

◆ Salt is mentioned almost 30 times in the Bible, but there is no mention of pepper.

◆ The longest name in the Bible is Maher-shalal-hash-baz (Isaiah 8:1). It means 'quick to the plunder, fast to the prey'. (No words in the Bible are more than six syllables long.)

◆ The shortest personal names are No (Jeremiah 46:25), Og

(Deuteronomy 31:4) and So (2 Kings 17:4). The shortest place names are Ai (Genesis 13:3), Ar (Deuteronomy 2:9), Ed (Joshua 23:34), On (Genesis 41:45), and Ur (Genesis 11:28). Uz is both a personal name (Genesis 10:23) and a place name (Job 1:1).

◆ No verse of the Bible contains all the letters of the alphabet, but some come close: Ezra 7:21 contains all the letters of the alphabet except j; Galatians 1:14 contains all the letters except k; Joshua 7:24 contains all the letters except q, as do 1 Kings 1:9, 1 Chronicles 12:40, 2 Chronicles 36:10, Ezekiel 28:13, Daniel 4:37 and Haggai 1:1; 1 Chronicles 4:10 contains all the letters except x.

◆ It is said that the Bible can be read aloud from beginning to end in about 70 hours.

◆ Many of the Bible statistics that are quoted, in this book and elsewhere, originate in the Introduction to the Critical Study of the Holy Scriptures by Thomas Hartwell Horne (1780–1862), an English librarian and Anglican priest.

CHAPTER AND VERSE

The chapters and verses of the modern Bible are not part of the original texts. The system of dividing the Bible into chapters was first introduced into the Latin version of the Bible by Stephen Langton (died 1228), an Englishman who was at the time a lecturer at the University of Paris and who later became a cardinal and Archbishop of Canterbury. This system was gradually adopted into Bibles written in other languages. Verses came later. Numbered verses for the Old Testament (the Jewish Bible) were first set out by a rabbi, Isaac Nathan, about the middle of the 14th century, and the system of verses for the New Testament was created by Robert Estienne, a French printer who used it in a Greek New Testament published in 1551. The first complete Bible printed with the verse divisions we have today was a Latin version printed by Estienne in 1555. The first English Bible to have the verse divisions was a New Testament printed in 1557 and the first complete Bible to have them was printed in 1560, both in Geneva.

The principle behind Estienne's verse divisions is not clear, as he sometimes makes a split in the middle of a sentence. According to Estienne's son, Estienne made the divisions while on a journey from Paris to Lyons. Some people have suggested that he marked the start of a new verse every time his horse jolted his hand!

BIBLE LANGUAGES

The Bible was written in three languages. The Old Testament was written mostly in Hebrew (the language of the Israelites and of modern-day Israel), with some passages in Aramaic (a language related to Hebrew that came to be widely spoken throughout the Middle East and was one of the official languages of the Assyrian empire).

The New Testament is written in the everyday Greek of the 1st and 2nd centuries AD, called the Koine (from Greek *koinos* meaning 'common').

Aramaic in the Bible

In Genesis 31:47–48, Jacob gives the memorial heap of stones a Hebrew name 'Galeed' but Laban, from Haran, gives it an Aramaic name 'Jegar-sahadutha'. Jeremiah 10:11, Ezra 4:8–6:18 and 7:12–26, and Daniel 2:4–7:28) are in Aramaic, not Hebrew.

In the New Testament, Jesus' words are sometimes given in Aramaic:
Talitha, cumi (Mark 5:41) = 'Little girl, get up.'
Eloi, Eloi, lama sabachthani? (Mark 15:34) 'My God, My God, why hast thou forsaken me?'

Simon's nickname *Cephas* 'the rock' is from Aramaic *kepha*. Also *Golgotha* = 'the skull' = Calvary and *bar* meaning 'son of' in names: Simon Bar-Jona (= Simon Peter; Matthew 16:17), Barabbas (= 'son of Abba'), Barnabas, Bartholomew, Bartimaeus. (The Hebrew equivalent is *ben*.)

Abba (Romans 8:15 and Galatians 4:6) is Aramaic for 'father', and *maranatha* (1 Corinthians 16:22) means 'Come, O Lord'.

BIBLE TRANSLATION

The first full translation of the Bible into English was made by John Wycliffe and his assistants in the late 14th century. Much of the present-day work of Bible translation is carried out by the Wycliffe Bible Translators, an organization founded in 1942 by a Christian missionary, William Cameron Townsend, and named after John Wycliffe. According to the Wycliffe Bible Translators' statistics up to June 2007, of the nearly 7,000 languages in the world, some or all of the Bible has now been translated into 2,426: 429 languages have the Bible, 1,144 languages have the New Testament, and there is some part of the Bible in a further 853 languages. Another organization involved in Bible translation is the United Bible Societies.

A shorthand New Testament was published in about 1665. A Pitman shorthand version of the Bible was published in 1904.

THE BIBLE IN THE LANGUAGES OF EUROPE

The Bible has been translated into more than 40 European languages. These are the dates of some of the earliest translations:

GERMAN **1466** ❖ ITALIAN **1471** ❖ CATALAN **1478** ❖ CZECH **1488** ❖ DUTCH **1526** ❖ FRENCH **1530** ❖ SWEDISH **1541** ❖ DANISH **1550** ❖ SPANISH **1553** ❖ POLISH **1561** ❖ ICELANDIC **1584** ❖ SLOVENIAN **1584** ❖ WELSH **1588** ❖ HUNGARIAN **1590** ❖ FINNISH **1642** ❖ IRISH **1685** ❖ ROMANIAN **1688** ❖ LATVIAN **1689** ❖ MANX **1733** ❖ LITHUANIAN **1735** ❖ ESTONIAN **1739** ❖ PORTUGUESE **1751** ❖ GAELIC **1801** ❖ SERBO-CROAT **1804** ❖ SLOVAK **1832** ❖ NORWEGIAN **1834** ❖ GREEK **1840** ❖ BASQUE **1865** ❖ BRETON **1866** ❖ BULGARIAN **1871** ❖ RUSSIAN **1875** ❖ UKRAINIAN **1903** ❖ BYELORUSSIAN **1973** ❖ MACEDONIAN **1990**

BIBLES OLD AND NEW

SOME IMPORTANT EDITIONS OF THE BIBLE

✟ *The* **Douai Bible** *is a translation of the Vulgate made by English Roman Catholic scholars at the English College at Douai, France, in the late 16th century.*

✟ *The* **Geneva Bible** *is a translation of the Bible made by English Protestants in Geneva, Switzerland, in the mid-16th century.*

✟ *In the 16th century, William Tyndale set out to produce an English translation that would let 'the boy that driveth the plough' understand the Bible. He was executed for heresy in 1536, but Tyndale's Bible had a great influence on the English of the Authorized Version.*

✟ *The* **Great Bible** *was an edition of the Bible authorized by King Henry VIII for use in the Church of England. It was published in 1539. It is called 'Great' because of its large size (with pages 9 inches by 15 inches or 23 x 38cm). A revised version of this, published in 1568, was known as the* **Bishops' Bible.**

✟ *The* **Septuagint** *is the Greek translation of the Hebrew Bible (= the Old Testament) made in Egypt in the 3rd and 2nd centuries* BC. *'Septuagint', often abbreviated LXX, comes from Latin* **septuaginta,** *meaning 'seventy'. According to legend, 72 translators, six from each of the Twelve Tribes of Israel, all separately made a translation of the whole Bible, and all 72 versions were identical. The Septuagint was the version of the Old Testament used by most early Christian communities. It includes several books not found in the Hebrew Bible (see page 152).*

✟ *The* **Vulgate** *is the Latin translation of the Bible made by St Jerome, completed in 405. 'Vulgate' comes from Latin* vulgata editio, *meaning the 'edition for general circulation'. In 1546, the Roman Catholic Council of Trent decreed that the Vulgate was the sole authoritative Latin version of the Bible.*

THE AUTHORIZED VERSION

The **Authorized Version** or **King James Version** of the Bible is a revision of the Bishops' Bible begun in 1604 and completed in 1611 for King James I of England. Many Christians still prefer to use this translation.

The edition was prepared by about 50 academics and churchmen, divided into six groups, two based in Oxford University, two in Cambridge University and two in Westminster. Each group worked on one section of the Bible: Genesis to Kings (Westminster); Chronicles to Ecclesiastes (Cambridge); Isaiah to Malachi (Oxford); the Gospels, Acts and Revelation (Oxford); Romans to Jude (Westminster) and the Apocrypha (Cambridge). Twelve of the translators then revised the whole text.

Their instructions were to follow the Bishops' Bible as far as possible, and modify it only where necessary. Their aim, as they themselves stated, was not to make a new translation nor to make a bad one into a good one, but to 'make a good one better, or out of many good ones, one principal good one'. It has been calculated that the Authorized Version derived about 60% of its text from its predecessors. It has been called 'the noblest monument of English prose'.

The English Bible – a book which, if everything else in our language should perish, would alone suffice to show the whole extent of its beauty and power.
Thomas Macaulay

Whatever merit there is in whatever I have written is simply due to that fact that when I was a child my mother daily read me a part of the Bible and daily made me learn a part of it by heart.
John Ruskin

Intense study of the Bible will keep any writer from being vulgar, in point of style.
Samuel Taylor Coleridge

The Gutenberg Bible

The first printed book using movable type was an edition of the Vulgate produced by Johannes Gutenberg in Mainz, Germany, and completed about 1456. It used Gutenberg's materials but was not published by him. It is also called the Forty-Two-Line Bible because it is printed in pages of two columns of 42 lines.

Thirty-five copies of Gutenberg's Bible were printed on parchment, for which some 5,950 calfskins would have been needed. Other copies were printed on paper.

SOME CURRENT EDITIONS OF THE BIBLE
AND THEIR ABBREVIATIONS

Some of these refer to the same version of the Bible (e.g. KJV = AV, GNT = GNB)

Amplified Bible ..... **Amp**	*New English Bible* ..... **NEB**
Authorized Version ..... **AV**	*New English Translation* ..... **NET**
Contemporary English Version ..... **CEV**	*New International Reader's Version* .... **NIrV**
Defined King James Version ..... **DKJV**	*New International Version* ..... **NIV**
English Standard Version ..... **ESV**	*New Jerusalem Bible* ..... **NJB**
God's Word ..... **GW**	*New King James Version* ..... **NKJV**
Good News Bible ..... **GNB**	*New Life Version* ..... **NLF**
Good News Translation ..... **GNT**	*New Living Translation* ..... **NLT**
Holman Christian Standard Bible .... **HCSB**	*New Revised Standard Version* ..... **NRSV**
International Standard Version ..... **ISV**	*New World Translation* ..... **NWT**
Jerusalem Bible ..... **JB**	*Phillip's New Testament in Modern*
King James 2000 ..... **KJ2000**	*English* .....*no abbreviation*
King James Version ..... **KJV**	*Revised English Bible* ..... **REB**
21st Century King James Version **KJ21**	*Revised Standard Version* ..... **RSV**
Literal translation of the Holy Bible.... **LITV**	*The Living Bible* ..... **TLB**
Modern King James Version ..... **MKJV**	*The Message* ..... **TM**
Moffatt Bible ..... *no abbreviation*	*Third Millennium Bible* ..... **TMB**
New American Bible ..... **NAB**	*Today's New International Version*.... **TNIV**
New American Standard Bible ..... **NASB**	*World English Bible* ..... **WEB**
New Century Version ..... **NCV**	

BIBLES WITH NICKNAMES

The Geneva Bible (see page 15) is also known as the **Breeches Bible,** because Genesis 3:7 says that Adam and Eve sewed fig-leaves together to make themselves breeches. (The King James Version has 'aprons'.)

✱

Miles Coverdale's 1535 translation of the Bible is known as the **Bug Bible.** At Psalm 91:5 it has 'Thou shalt not nede to be afrayed for eny bugges by night'. (The King James Version has 'terror'.)

✱

Inevitably, over the years, some editions of the Bible have been printed with errors in them. Many of these, too, have been given particular nicknames:

✱

The **Camels Bible**, published in 1823, is so called because Genesis 24:62 reads 'And Rebekah arose, and her camels' instead of 'and her damsels'.

✱

In the **Denial Bible** of 1792, Jesus says that it will be Philip, not Peter, who will deny him three times (Luke 22:34).

✱

In the 1810 edition of the Bible known as the **Ears to ear Bible,** Matthew 13:43 has 'Who hath ears to ear, let him hear' instead of 'ears to hear'.

The **Fool Bible** was published during the reign of Charles I (1625–49). At Psalm 14:1, it reads 'The fool hath said in his heart there is a God' instead of 'there is no God'. The printers were fined £3,000 for this mistake.

✱

In the **Forgotten Sins Bible** of 1638, Luke 7:47 has 'Her sins, which are many, are forgotten' instead of 'are forgiven'.

✱

Editions of the Geneva Bible published between 1608 and 1611 are known as the **Judas Bible** because they have 'Judas' instead of 'Jesus' addressing the disciples at John 6:67.

✱

An edition of the Bible printed in 1795 has 'Let the children first be killed' at Mark 7:27. It should of course be 'filled'.

There are many printing errors in the **Lions Bible**, published in 1804, but it takes its name from the misprint at 1 Kings 8:19, which reads 'thy son that shall come forth out of thy lions' instead of 'out of thy loins'.

∗

In the 1801 **Murderers Bible**, 'murmurers' was replaced by 'murderers' at Jude 16.

∗

One wonders what the printers were thinking of when they made this mistake: in the early-18th-century **Printers Bible**, the psalmist complains that 'printers have persecuted me without a cause' (Psalm 119:161); the word should be 'princes'.

∗

In the **'Sin on' Bible**, John 5:15 reads 'sin on more' instead of 'sin no more'.

∗

Reading the **Unrighteous Bible** of 1653, you would be surprised to learn at 1 Corinthians 6:9 that it is 'the unrighteous' who shall inherit the Kingdom of God'. It should, of course, be 'the righteous'.

The 1966 edition of the *Jerusalem Bible* accidentally omitted an *r* and so had the psalmist asking that people 'pay' for the peace of Jerusalem instead of 'pray' (Psalm 122:6).

∗

The word 'not' was omitted from the seventh commandment (Exodus 20:14) in the **Wicked Bible**. The commandment therefore reads 'Thou shalt commit adultery'. For this error the printers were fined £300. This Bible is also known as the **Adulterous Bible**.

∗

In the 1810 **Wife-hater Bible**, Luke 14:26 reads 'If any man come to me, and hate not his father, and mother, and wife, and children, and brethren, and sisters, yea, and his own wife also, he cannot be my disciple'. Jesus is not making a particular issue here about hating one's wife by repeating himself: what he said was 'and his own life also'.

BIBLES GREAT AND SMALL

One of the world's largest Bibles is the Codex Gigas, which dates from the early 13th century. It measures 36 × 20 inches (92 × 50.5 cm), and weighs 165 lb (75 kg), and the vellum needed for its pages is estimated to have used the skin of 160 donkeys. Its 624 pages contain the Old and New Testaments as well as formulas to treat diseases and uncover thieves. It is known as the Devil's Bible because legend has it that it was written by a monk in a single night with the aid of the Devil (historians estimate it really took up to 20 years). According to legend, a monk, sentenced to be walled up and die a slow death for some heinous sin, promised to write out the world's biggest Bible in return for his freedom. With just one night to produce it, he enlisted the help of the Devil. One of the two pages on show features a drawing of the Devil, and it is said that this drawing is the scribe's tribute to the role Satan played in the Bible's creation. Written around 1229, it was looted by Swedish soldiers from Prague Castle at the end of the Thirty Years War in 1648 and taken to Stockholm.

Another very large Bible is a copy of the King James Version which was created by Louis Waynai of Los Angeles in 1930 using a large home-made rubber stamp press. Mr Waynai is said to have devoted more than 8,700 hours of work to the task. The book has 8,048 pages and weighs 1,094 pounds (496 kg). When laid open, it measures 43½ inches tall and 98 inches wide (110 × 250 cm); when it is closed, the spine is 34 inches (86 cm) thick.

The New York Times of 30 April 1853 reported a Bible in the University of Göttingen written on 5,476 palm leaves.

There are various Bibles that claim to be the 'smallest ever', and modern technology is of course constantly allowing ever greater miniaturization, whether on paper or on other media.

Perhaps the smallest complete Bible ever printed was produced by Glasgow University Press and issued in 1896 by David Bryce & Son of Glasgow, Scotland and Henry Frowde of London. With a page size about 1⅝ × 1⅛ inches (4 × 2.8 cm), it contains 876 pages and is less than half an inch thick. It was packaged in a case, in which was included a magnifying glass to help readers decipher the tiny print. 25,000 copies were printed.

Nanotechnology has of course allowed even greater miniaturization than is possible on paper. One 1,600-page version of the Bible is available on a screen the size of a matchbox. (The letters are 0.0002 inches high, and the Bible is read by means of a 100 × magnifier.) There is another company that can reproduce the whole Bible on a small crystal. And yet another version of the Bible, in Greek, has been printed on a crystal less than an inch (20 mm) in diameter.

What is claimed to be the world's smallest Hebrew Bible (= the Christian Old Testament) was created in 2007 by scientists at Israel's Technion Institute of Technology. Using particle beams, they managed to etch the more than 300,000 words of the Hebrew Bible on to a gold-coated silicon chip 0.5 mm square (which is smaller than the head of a pin).

WHAT PEOPLE HAVE SAID ABOUT THE BIBLE

ON THE VALUE OF THE BIBLE:

I have found in it words for my inmost thoughts, songs for my joy, utterance for my hidden griefs, and pleadings for my shame and feebleness.
Samuel Taylor Coleridge, English poet

♦

I believe that the existence of the Bible is the greatest benefit to the human race. Any attempt to belittle it ... is a crime against humanity.
Immanuel Kant, German philosopher

♦

The Bible is worth all other books that have ever been printed.
Patrick Henry, American statesman

The first and almost only book deserving of universal attention is the Bible.
John Quincy Adams, American statesman

♦

How great and glorious it is to have the Word of God!
Martin Luther, German churchman

♦

The Bible is the sceptre by which the Heavenly King rules His Church.
John Calvin, French churchman

♦

The Bible, the whole Bible, and nothing but the Bible is the religion of Christ's Church.
Charles Spurgeon, English churchman

♦

The scriptures teach us the best way of living, the noblest way of suffering, and the most comfortable way of dying.
John Flavel, English churchman

ON THE BIBLE AND GOOD GOVERNMENT:

The Bible is for the Government of the People, by the People, and for the People.
Prologue to John Wycliffe's translation of the Bible (1384)

♦

That book accounts for the supremacy of England.
Queen Victoria

♦

It is impossible to rightly govern the world ... without the Bible.
George Washington, American statesman

22

That Book is the rock on which our Republic rests.

Andrew Jackson, American statesman

ON THE TRUSTWORTHINESS OF THE BIBLE:

I find more sure marks of authenticity in the Bible than in any profane history whatsoever. No sciences are better attested than the religion of the Bible.

Sir Isaac Newton, English scientist

ON THE BIBLE AND EDUCATION:

A thorough knowledge of the Bible is worth more than a college education.

Theodore Roosevelt, American statesman

◆

Bible reading is an education in itself.

Alfred, Lord Tennyson, English poet

◆

Education is useless without the Bible.

Noah Webster, American writer and educationist

UNFAVOURABLE OPINIONS OF THE BIBLE:

There is much in the Bible against which every instinct of my being rebels, so much that I regret the necessity which has compelled me to read it through from beginning to end. I do not think that the knowledge which I have gained of its history and sources compensates me for the unpleasant details it has forced upon my attention.

Helen Keller, American writer

◆

We have used the Bible as if it were a mere special constable's handbook, an opium dose for keeping beasts of burden patient while they are overloaded.

Charles Kingsley, English writer and clergyman

◆

Whenever we read the obscene stories, the voluptuous debaucheries, the cruel and torturous executions, the unrelenting vindictiveness, with which more than half the Bible is filled, it would be more consistent that we called it the word of a demon than the Word of God.

Thomas Paine, American radical writer and activist

Names for the Bible

The Bible, the Holy Bible; the Book, the Good Book, the Book of Books; Scripture, the Scriptures, Holy Writ; the Word, the Word of God.

... AND WHAT THE BIBLE SAYS ABOUT ITSELF

God is not a man, that he should lie: ... hath he said, and shall he not do it? or hath he spoken, and shall he not make it good? (Numbers 23:19)

Man doth not live by bread only, but by every word that proceedeth out of the mouth of the Lord doth man live. (Deuteronomy 8:3)

Thy word is a lamp unto my feet, and a light unto my path. (Psalm 119:105)

Thy word is true from the beginning: and every one of thy righteous judgments endureth for ever. (Psalm 119:160)

The grass withereth, the flower fadeth: but the word of our God shall stand for ever. (Isaiah 40:8)

Is not my word like as a fire? saith the Lord; and like a hammer that breaketh the rock in pieces? (Jeremiah 23:29)

For verily I say unto you, Till heaven and earth pass, one jot or one tittle shall in no wise pass from the law, till all be fulfilled. (Matthew 5:18)

Heaven and earth shall pass away, but my words shall not pass away. (Matthew 24:35)

The sword of the Spirit, which is the word of God. (Ephesians 3:16)

All scripture is given by inspiration of God, and is profitable for doctrine, for reproof, for correction, for instruction in righteousness: that the man of God may be perfect, thoroughly furnished unto all good works. (2 Timothy 3:16)

For the word of God is quick, and powerful, and sharper than any two-edged sword, piercing even to the dividing asunder of soul and spirit, and of the joints and marrow, and is a discerner of the thoughts and intents of the heart. (Hebrews 4:12)

But the word of the Lord endureth for ever. (1 Peter 1:25)

INTERPRETING THE BIBLE

I believe that the Bible is to be understood and received in the plain and obvious meaning of its passages; for I cannot persuade myself that a book intended for the instruction and conversion of the whole world should cover its true meaning in any such mystery and doubt that none but critics and philosophers can discover it.

Daniel Webster, American writer and educationist

The four levels of meaning

Not all those who have studied the Bible have shared Webster's opinion. Some have argued that in addition to the 'plain and obvious meaning', there are other hidden meanings to be discovered. It has been suggested that there could be any of four types or levels of meaning in a text.

✦ The **literal** meaning is Webster's 'plain and obvious meaning', in which words are understood in their everyday senses and what is read is taken at face value.

✦ The **moral** meaning of a text is the way in which what the text says can be understood as relevant to our own lives and situations and to the decisions we make.

✦ The **allegorical** meaning involves the interpretation of the elements of the text as standing for something else.

✦ The **spiritual** meaning of a text is a hidden, inner, often mystical meaning.

ALLEGORY IN INTERPRETING THE BIBLE

Some Jewish and Christian teachers were particularly keen on reading allegorical meanings into the Scriptures. For example, the love poems of the Song of Solomon were interpreted allegorically as representing the love between God and Israel or between Christ and the Church. Employing allegory, St Augustine wrote that the garden of Eden signifies the church, its four rivers the four gospels, its fruit trees the saints, and their fruit the good works of the saints. The tree of life is Christ.

The reformers Martin Luther and John Calvin did not approve of allegorical interpretations of Scripture. Allegories, said Luther, are empty speculations. To allegorize is to juggle with Scripture. And Calvin alleged that it was Satan himself who had introduced allegory into Church teaching 'for the purpose of rendering the doctrine of Scripture ambiguous and destitute of all certainty and firmness.'

TYPOLOGY

Typology involves interpreting a person or event in the Old Testament as symbolically foreshadowing a person or event in the New Testament, such as Adam in the Old Testament and Christ in the New Testament. Hebrews 9 relates the actions of the high priest to that of Jesus as saviour, and the Mosaic covenant and the new covenant in Jesus' blood. In 1 Peter 3, Peter teaches that the water of the Flood symbolizes the water of baptism.

KABBALAH

Kabbalah means 'tradition' in Hebrew. It denotes a Jewish system of mystical interpretation of the Bible, especially the Torah (see page 62), to extract meanings and predictions hidden in the text. Like the system on page 25, kabbalah recognizes four levels of meaning in a text, and it concentrates on the fourth level, the hidden spiritual meaning. A key text is the 13th-century *Sefer ha-Zofar*, the 'Book of Splendour' in which are discussed mystical and symbolic meanings of the Torah, the Song of Solomon and the Book of Ruth, and also the nature of God, the origin of the universe and the problem of evil.

Gematria

Each letter of the Hebrew alphabet has a numerical value (for example, aleph = 1, beth = 2, yod = 10, tav = 400). Gematria involves the interpretation of Scripture by exploring the relationships between words or phrases that have the same numerical value when the values of their individual letters are added together, or substituting one word or phrase for another of the same value. Only consonants count.

Aleph	*a*	1
Beth	*b*	2
Gimel	*g*	3
Daleth	*d*	4
He	*h*	5
Vav	*v*	6
Zayin	*z*	7
Cheth	*ch*	8
Teth	*t*	9
Yod	*y*	10
Kaph	*k*	20
Lamed	*l*	30
Mem	*m*	40
Nun	*n*	50
Samech	*s*	60
Ayin	*e*	70
Pe	*p*	80
Tzade	*tz*	90
Koph	*k*	100
Resh	*r*	200
Shin	*sh*	300
Tav	*t*	400

Examples of gematria

At Genesis 28:12, we are told that Jacob dreamed of a ladder stretching up to heaven. The Hebrew word for 'ladder' in gematria has a numerical value of 130. This is the same as the numerical value of 'Sinai'. On this basis, it is argued that the Law revealed to Moses at Sinai is mankind's path to heaven. Similarly, the name 'David' has a value of 14, and in Matthew's gospel Jesus's ancestors are listed in three groups of 14.

Gematria may be applied to other languages such as Greek, Latin or English. In English the 26 letters of the alphabet generally have the values 1 to 26, which gives, for example, a sum of 74 for both 'Jesus' and 'Messiah'.

The Hebrew alphabet

One well-known example of the use of gematria is in the interpretation of '666', the 'number of the beast' in Revelation 13:18 to refer to the Roman Emperor Nero. When the letters of the Greek for 'Caesar Nero' are replaced by Hebrew letters, you get a formula that could be transcribed qsr nrwn. If these letters are then given their numerical equivalents in gematria (100 - 60 - 200 - 50 - 200 - 6 - 50) and added together, you get the number 666. (See also page 192.)

USES FOR THE BIBLE

Bibliomancy

Bibliomancy is the practice of foretelling the future by means of a randomly chosen passage in a book. The book chosen is very often the Bible, in order to receive a message from God. One method is to close your eyes and open the Bible at random or else balance it on its spine and allow it to fall open. Still with your eyes closed, you put your finger somewhere on the open page, and so select the passage to read.

WITCHES AND THE BIBLE

In the Middle Ages a person suspected of witchcraft might be weighed on a huge set of scales against the large, heavy Bible from the local church. If the suspect weighed more than the Bible, he or she was free; if they were found to be lighter than the Bible, this was taken as evidence of their guilt. There is a record of this test being carried out on an old woman as late as 1759 at Aylesbury.

FINDING A THIEF

One ancient method of proving a suspect to be a thief involved using a Bible and a key. The suspect's name was inserted into the hollow end of the key which was then placed in a Bible while Psalm 50, verse 18 was recited:

When thou sawest a thief, then thou consentedst with him, and hast been partaker with adulterers. If the person whose name was in the key was the thief, the key would turn round.

An innocent hiding place

Over the years many things have been hidden between the covers of a hollowed-out Bible, such as guns and drugs. In one recent case, Canadian border officials discovered the drugs because they noticed that the Bibles were heavier than they should be. In another case, a young woman tried to smuggle marijuana in Bibles to her boyfriend in prison.

THE BIBLE IN THE ARTS

POETRY

JOHN MILTON *Paradise Lost* (1667) – about Adam and Eve and the Fall; *Paradise Regained* (1671) – about Jesus ❖ CHRISTOPHER SMART *A Song to David* (1763) ❖ LORD BYRON *Cain* (1821) ❖ ROBERT MONTGOMERY *The Messiah* (1832) ❖ R W DIXON *Christ's Company* (1861) – about Mary Magdalene, John, etc ❖ HENRY W LONGFELLOW *Christus: A Mystery* (1872) ❖ T S ELIOT *The Journey of the Magi* (1930)

In *Paradise Lost*, Milton coined the word 'Pandemonium' (= 'the place of all demons') as the name of the capital of Hell.

BOOKS

LEW WALLACE *Ben Hur* (1880) ❖ HENRY ADAMS *Esther* (1884) ❖ HENRY SIENKIEWICZ *Quo Vadis?* (1896) – about Peter ❖ SHOLEM ASCH *The Nazarene* (1939); *The Apostle* (1943) – about Paul; *Mary* (1949); *Moses* (1951) ❖ LLOYD C DOUGLAS *The Robe* (1942) – the Crucifixion; *The Fisherman* (1949) – Peter ❖ ROBERT GRAVES *King Jesus* (1946) ❖ ARCHIBALD MACLEISH *J.B.* (1958) – Job ❖ TAYLOR CALDWELL *Dear and Glorious Physician* (1959) – about Luke the gospel-writer ❖ JAMES BRIDIE *Jonah and the Whale* (1968) ❖ MARJORIE HOLMES *Two from Galilee* (1972) – Mary and Joseph ❖ NIKOS KAZANTZAKIS *The Last Temptation of Christ* (1988)

'Quo vadis?' is a Latin phrase meaning 'Where are you going?'. There is a legend that when Peter was fleeing imprisonment and possible death in Rome, he met Jesus heading towards the city. 'Where are you going, Lord?' said Peter. 'I am going to Rome to be crucified again,' said Jesus. 'Then I'm going with you,' said Peter, and turned back to meet his death.

PLAYS AND MUSICALS

JOHN MILTON *Samson Agonistes* (1671) – the death of Samson ❖ HENRY W LONGFELLOW *The Divine Tragedy* (1871) – the life of Jesus ❖ GEORGE CABOT LODGE *Cain* (1904) ❖ SHOLEM ASCH *Jephthah's Daughter* (1915) ❖ EUGENE O'NEILL *Belshazzar* (1915); *Lazarus Laughed* (1925) ❖ GEORGE MOORE *The Brook Kerith* (1916) – Jesus after the crucifixion ❖ THORNTON WILDER *Now the Servant's Name was Malchus* (1928) – the arrest of Jesus; *Hast Thou Considered My Servant Job?* (1928) – Jesus, Satan and Judas ❖ MARC CONNELLY *Green Pastures* (1929) – various Bible stories ❖ DOROTHY L SAYERS *He That Should Come* (1940) – the Nativity ❖ *The Man Born to Be King* (1942) – the life of Jesus ❖ CHRISTOPHER FRY *A Sleep of Prisoners* (1951) – Cain and Abel, Abraham and Isaac, David and Absalom, and Shadrach, Meshach and Abed-nego. ❖ TIM RICE & ANDREW LLOYD WEBBER *Joseph and the Amazing Technicolor Dreamcoat* (1968) ❖ *Jesus Christ Superstar* (1970) ❖ STEPHEN SCHWARTZ & JOHN-MICHAEL TEBELAK *Godspell* (1970) – Matthew's gospel

FILMS

CECIL B DEMILLE *The Ten Commandments* (1923) – with Theodore Roberts as Moses; *The King of Kings* (1927) – with H. B. Warner as Jesus; *The Ten Commandments* (1956) – with Charlton Heston as Moses ❖ MERVIN LEROY *Quo Vadis?* (1951) – with Robert Taylor as a Roman military commander, Deborah Kerr as a Christian girl, Peter Ustinov as Nero, and Finlay Currie as Peter ❖ HENRY KOSTER *The Robe* (1953) – with Richard Burton as the centurion who crucified Jesus ❖ FRANK BORZAGE *The Big Fisherman* (1959) – with Howard Keel as Peter ❖ WILLIAM WYLER *Ben-Hur* (1959) – with Charlton Heston as Ben-Hur ❖ NICHOLAS RAY *King of Kings* (1961) – with Jeffrey Hunter as Jesus ❖ PIER PAOLO PASOLINI *The Gospel According to Saint Matthew* (1964) – with Enrique Irazoqui as Jesus ❖ GEORGE STEVENS *The Greatest Story Ever Told* (1965) – with Max von Sydow as Jesus, Charlton Heston as John the Baptist, and John Wayne as a Roman centurion ❖ MARTIN SCORSESE *The Last Temptation of Christ* (1988) – with William Dafoe as Jesus ❖ MEL GIBSON *The Passion of the Christ* (2004) – with James Caviezel as Jesus

PEOPLE OF THE BIBLE

From Aaron to Zuzim:

AARON Brother of Moses

ABED-NEGO One of Daniel's companions in Babylon

ABEL Second son of Adam and Eve; murdered by his brother Cain

ABRAHAM The patriarch to whose descendants God promised the land of Canaan

ADAM The first man

AHAB 7th king of northern Israel; husband of Jezebel

AMOS 8th-century BC prophet

ANDREW One of the apostles; brother of Simon Peter

ASHER Son of Jacob; patriarch of Israelite tribe

BALAAM Prophet hired to curse the Israelites; famous for having a talking donkey

BARABBAS Bandit freed by Pontius Pilate in place of Jesus

BARNABAS Apostle; companion of Paul

BARTHOLOMEW Apostle

BATHSHEBA Wife of King David after the death of her husband Uriah; mother of King Solomon

BELSHAZZAR King of Babylon, 539BC; according to the Book of Daniel, son of Nebuchadnezzar, but in fact son of a later king, Nabonidus

BENJAMIN Son of Jacob; patriarch of Israelite tribe

BOAZ Wealthy landowner in Bethlehem; husband of Ruth and great-grandfather of King David

CAIAPHAS Jewish high priest at the trial of Jesus

CAIN First son of Adam and Eve; murdered his brother Abel

CALEB Israelite leader; like Joshua, faithful to God

CORNELIUS The first non-Jewish convert to Christianity

DANIEL Prophet famed for surviving a night in a den of lions; Babylonian name: Belteshazzar

DAVID Second king of Israel; killed the giant Goliath

DEBORAH Prophetess; one of the Israelite judges

DELILAH Philistine woman who seduced Samson into giving away the secret of his strength

ELI Israelite priest

ELIJAH 9th-century BC prophet

ELISHA 9th-century BC prophet

ELIZABETH Mother of John the Baptist

ENOCH ❶ Son of Cain ❷ Father of Methuselah

EPHRAIM Son of Joseph; patriarch of Israelite tribe

ESAU Son of Isaac; brother of Jacob

ESTHER Jewish girl who became queen of Persia

EVE The first woman, wife of Adam

EZEKIEL 6th-century BC prophet

EZRA Jewish scribe sent to Jerusalem to teach the Jewish Law

GABRIEL Angel who interprets Daniel's vision and who tells Mary that she will bear a son Jesus

GAD Son of Jacob; patriarch of Israelite tribe

GAMALIEL Jewish rabbi, teacher of Paul

GIDEON Judge of Israel

GOLIATH Philistine giant killed by David

HABAKKUK 7th-century BC prophet

HAGAR Servant of Sarah; given to Abraham as a wife; mother of Ishmael

HAGGAI 6th-century BC prophet

HAM Son of Noah; father of Canaan; causes Noah to curse Canaan

HANNAH Mother of the prophet Samuel

HEROD Name of family of Jewish rulers

HIRAM King of Tyre, 10th century BC; friend to David and Solomon

HOSEA 8th-century BC prophet

ISAAC Son of Abraham and Sarah

ISAIAH 8th-century BC prophet

ISHMAEL Son of Abraham by Hagar

ISRAEL Name given to Jacob, the ancestor of the Twelve Tribes of Israel

ISSACHAR Son of Jacob; patriarch of Israelite tribe

JACOB Son of Isaac and Rebekah; brother of Esau

JAIRUS Ruler of the synagogue in Capernaum whose daughter was healed by Jesus

JAMES ❶ Brother of John, son of Zebedee; an apostle ❷ Son of

Alphaeus; an apostle

JAPHETH Son of Noah

JEPHTHAH Judge of Israel; obliged to kill his own daughter to fulfil a vow

JEREMIAH 7th- to 6th-century BC prophet

JEROBOAM First king of the northern kingdom of Israel after Solomon's kingdom split

JESSE Father of King David

JETHRO Father-in-law of Moses

JEZEBEL Wife of King Ahab; her name became a byword for a shameless, immoral woman

JOB A righteous man who suffers undeserved misfortune

JOEL 8th-century BC prophet

JOHN Brother of James, son of Zebedee; an apostle

JOHN THE BAPTIST Forerunner of Jesus

JONAH Prophet hero of a story in which he is swallowed by a large fish

JONATHAN Son of King Saul and friend to David

JOSEPH ❶ Son of Jacob; father of Ephraim and Manasseh ❷ Husband of Mary the mother of Jesus ❸ (Joseph of Arimathea) A Jew who was a secret follower of Jesus; provided his own tomb for the burial of Jesus

JOSHUA Israelite leader after Moses; led the conquest of Canaan

JUDAH Son of Jacob; patriarch of Israelite tribe

JUDAS ❶ Apostle ❷ Brother of Jesus; possibly wrote the Letter of Jude ❸ (Judas Iscariot) The apostle who betrayed Jesus

LAZARUS ❶ Brother of Martha and Mary; raised from the dead by Jesus ❷ A beggar in a parable of Jesus

LOT Abraham's nephew; his wife was turned into a pillar of salt as they fled from Sodom

LUKE Author of a gospel and the Acts of the Apostles

MALACHI 5th-century BC prophet

MANASSEH Son of Joseph; patriarch of Israelite tribe

MARK Author of a gospel

MARTHA Sister of Lazarus and Mary

MARY ❶ Mother of Jesus ❷ Sister of Martha and Lazarus ❸ (Mary Magdalene) Follower of Jesus; he cast demons out of her; she was the first to learn of the resurrection

MATTHEW Apostle and author of a gospel

MESHACH One of Daniel's companions in Babylon

METHUSELAH Grandfather of Noah; lived to the age of 969

MIRIAM Sister of Moses and Aaron

MOSES Israelite leader during the Exodus and the journey to Canaan

NAHUM 7th-century BC prophet

NAPHTALI Son of Jacob; patriarch of Israelite tribe

NATHANAEL Apostle

NEHEMIAH Jewish leader sent to restore Jerusalem and rebuild its walls

NOAH Patriarch who built the Ark and survived the Flood

OBADIAH 6th-century BC prophet

PAUL Great missionary apostle of the early Christian church

PETER Nickname of Simon the apostle, brother of Andrew

PHILEMON Recipient of a letter from Paul regarding Philemon's slave Onesimus

PHILIP ❶ Apostle ❷ Deacon of the early church

PONTIUS PILATE Roman governor who sentenced Jesus to crucifixion

RACHEL Second wife of Jacob; mother of Joseph and Benjamin

REBEKAH Wife of Isaac

REHOBOAM Son of Solomon; last king of united Israel and first king of the southern kingdom of Judah

REUBEN Son of Jacob; patriarch of Israelite tribe

RUTH Moabite girl who married Boaz; great-grandmother of David

SALOME Daughter of Herodias who danced for Herod and asked for the head of John the Baptist

SAMSON Judge of Israel noted for his strength, which he lost when his hair was cut

SAMUEL Prophet who anointed Saul king

SARAH Wife of Abraham; mother of Isaac

SAUL ❶ First king of Israel ❷ Hebrew name of Paul

SETH Third son of Adam and Eve

SHADRACH One of Daniel's companions in Babylon

SHEM Son of Noah

SIMEON Son of Jacob; patriarch of Israelite tribe

SIMON ❶ = Peter ❷ Apostle; a zealot ❸ (Simon of Cyrene) The man forced by the Romans to carry Jesus' cross

SOLOMON Third king of Israel; son of King David; noted for his wisdom

STEPHEN First Christian martyr

THOMAS Apostle; noted for his scepticism about the resurrection

TIMOTHY Companion of Paul

TITUS Companion of Paul

URIAH Soldier in David's army; husband of Bathsheba; David caused him to be killed in order to marry Bathsheba

ZEBEDEE Father of James and John

ZEBULUN Son of Jacob; patriarch of Israelite tribe

ZECHARIAH ❶ 6th-century BC prophet ❷ Father of John the Baptist

ZEPHANIAH 7th-century BC prophet

And the Zuzim? They were a people mentioned in Genesis 14.

WHAT'S IN A NAME?

NAMES INCLUDING YAH(WEH) AND EL, THE NAMES OF GOD

ADONIJAH *my lord is Yahweh*
AHAZIAH *Yahweh has grasped*
AMAZIAH *Yahweh is mighty*
ATHALIAH *Yahweh is exalted*
AZARIAH *Yahweh has helped*
ELIJAH *Yahweh is God*
HANANIAH *Yahweh has been gracious*
HEZEKIAH *Yahweh is my strength*
ISAIAH *Yahweh is salvation*
JEREMIAH *Yahweh lifts up* or *Yahweh loosens*
JOSIAH *may Yahweh give*
MICAH/MICAIAH *who is like Yahweh?*
NEHEMIAH *Yahweh has comforted*
OBADIAH *servant/worshipper of Yahweh*
PEKAHIAH *Yahweh has opened*
URIAH *Yahweh is my light*
ZECHARIAH *Yahweh remembers*
ZEDEKIAH *Yahweh is my righteousness*
ZEPHANIAH *Yahweh has hidden*

JEHOIACHIN *Yahweh will establish*
JEHOIADA *Yahweh knows*

JEHOIAKIM *Yahweh has established*
JEHORAM/JORAM *Yahweh is exalted*
JEHOSHAPHAT *Yahweh has judged*
JOAB *Yahweh is father*
JOASH *Yahweh has given*
JOCHEBED *Yahweh is glorious*
JOEL *Yahweh is God*
JOHANAN/JOHN *Yahweh is gracious*
JONATHAN *Yahweh has given*
JOSHUA/JESUS *Yahweh saves*

DANIEL *God is my judge*
EZEKIEL *God strengthens*
ELIZABETH *God is my oath*
GABRIEL *man of God* or *strength of God*
GAMALIEL *reward of God*
ISHMAEL *God hears*
ISRAEL *God strives* or *he struggles with God*
JOEL *Yahweh is God*
MICHAEL *who is like God?*
NATHANAEL *gift of God*
SAMUEL *name of God* or *heard by God*

MEANINGS OF SOME OTHER BIBLE NAMES

ABIGAIL *my father rejoices*
ABRAHAM *father of many*
ADAM *earth*
ANDREW *manly*
BARNABAS *son of comfort*
BARTHOLOMEW *son of Tolmai*
BENJAMIN *son of the right hand = 'lucky'*

DAVID *beloved*
DEBORAH *bee*
DELILAH *desired* or *delicate*
DINAH *avenged* or *judged*
DORCAS *gazelle*
ESTHER *star*
EVE *life*

GIDEON *hewer*
HANNAH/ANNA *grace*
ISAAC *he laughs*
JACOB/JAMES *follower*
JONAH *dove*
JOSEPH *he will add*
MARTHA *lady, mistress*
MARY/MIRIAM *bitterness* or *beloved*
MATTHEW *gift of Yahweh*
MELCHIZEDEK *king of righteousness*
MOSES **probably** *pulled out*
NAOMI *pleasant*
PAUL *little*
PETER *rock*

PHILIP *horse-lover*
RACHEL *ewe*
REBEKAH/REBECCA *noose*
RUTH *friend*
SALOME *peace*
SAUL *appointed*
SETH *appointed*
SOLOMON **probably** *peaceful*
STEPHEN *crown*
TABITHA *gazelle*
THOMAS *twin*
TIMOTHY *honoured by God*
ZEBEDEE *gift of God*

Names for the unnamed

Some unreliable traditions supply names for people not given names in the Bible itself:

❖ Potiphar's wife who tried to seduce Joseph is ZULEIKA
❖ the daughter of Pharaoh who adopted Moses is BITHIAH or THEBATIS
❖ Job has two wives – SITIS (or SITIDOS) and later DINAH
❖ Jephthah's daughter is SEILA
❖ the rich man who ignores the beggar Lazarus is named PHINEAS
❖ the woman Jesus heals of bleeding (Matthew 9) is BERNICE or JOSEPHIA
❖ Pilate's wife is named PROCLA/PROCULA, CLAUDIA or PERPETUA.

See also pages 94 (wives of the patriarchs), 156–7 (the shepherds and the Magi) and 184 (the crucified thieves).

Peoples of the Bible

AMALEKITES A people living to the south-west of the Dead Sea. Descendants of Amalek, grandson of Esau. Made frequent attacks on Israel; defeated by Joshua (Exodus 17), Saul (1 Samuel 15) and David (1 Samuel 30).

AMMONITES Descendants of Ben-Ammi, the younger son of Lot, living to the east of the Jordan. The Israelites were not to attack them (Deuteronomy 2:19), but there were conflicts with Israel and they were defeated by both Saul (1 Samuel 11) and David (2 Samuel 12).

AMORITES A people inhabiting Canaan and territory east of the Jordan later occupied by the tribes of Gad, Reuben and Manasseh.

ARAMEANS A people occupying territory in what is now Syria. Aram was a son of Shem. When Abraham left Ur, he and his family travelled to Haran, a city in Aram, before heading south through Canaan. Aramaic, a language related to Hebrew, became widely spoken throughout the Middle East.

CHALDEANS A people of southern Babylonia. King Nebuchadnezzar of Babylon was a Chaldean.

EDOMITES A people living to the south-east of the Dead Sea. Descendants of Esau. The Israelites were not to attack them (Deuteronomy 23:7–8), but there were conflicts with Israel and they were defeated by David (1 Kings 11:15–16) and Amaziah (2 Kings 14). Some Edomites later fled into Judaea; the Herods were of Edomite extraction.

ELAMITES Elam was a descendant of Shem. The country of Elam was on the east side of the River Tigris. Some of its people were transported to Samaria.

HITTITES The Hittites were a Canaanite people living around Hebron. They may have been unrelated to the Hittites who had a great empire further to the north. Abraham bought a field from a Hittite as a burying-ground. Esau married two Hittite women.

JEBUSITES   Descendants of the third son of Canaan. Jerusalem was their chief city, and was also known as Jebus.

MEDES   Media was a territory to the south-west of the Caspian Sea. The Medes were related to the Persians, who lived further south to the east of the Persian Gulf, and were conquered by them in 550BC.

MIDIANITES   A nomadic people living mainly to the south of the Edomites, east of the Red Sea. Midian was a son of Abraham. Midianites were closely associated with Ishmaelites, and it was they who sold Joseph to Potiphar (Genesis 37). Moses had a Midianite wife.

MOABITES   The Moabites lived to the north of the Edomites, on the east side of the Dead Sea. Moab was a son of Lot. It was a Moabite king who summoned Balaam to curse the Israelites (Numbers 22–24). David's great-grandmother Ruth was a Moabite girl.

PHILISTINES   Originally from the Aegean area, the Philistines occupied the coastal region directly opposite the Dead Sea. Palestine takes its name from the Philistines. Abraham and Isaac had dealings with a Philistine king, but when the Israelites left Egypt, they avoided entering Philistine territory. Samson married a Philistine girl, but also killed many Philistines. David killed the Philistine giant Goliath, but also fled from Saul to a Philistine king. The Philistines long had a monopoly in iron-working.

PHOENICIANS   Phoenicia was a coastal territory in what is now Lebanon. Two of its chief cities were Tyre and Sidon. King Hiram of Tyre was a friend to David and Solomon, and supplied the timber and craftsmen for the building of the Temple. The infamous Jezebel, wife of King Ahab of Israel, was a princess of Tyre and Sidon.

SOME OF THE NAMED HUSBANDS AND WIVES OF THE BIBLE

Adam – Eve ❖ Lamech – Adah, Zillah ❖ Abraham – Sarah, Keturah ❖ Isaac – Rebekah ❖ Jacob – Leah, Rachel ❖ Esau – Judith, Bashemath, Mahalath (or Adah, Aholibamah, Bashemath) ❖ Joseph – Asenath ❖ Moses – Zipporah ❖ Aaron – Elisheba ❖ Boaz – Ruth ❖ Saul – Ahinoam ❖ David – Michal, Abigail, Ahinoam, Maacah, Haggith, Abital, Eglah, Bathsheba ❖ Nabal – Abigail ❖ Solomon – Naamah ❖ Ahab – Jezebel ❖ Ahasuerus – Vashti, Esther ❖ Hosea – Gomer ❖ Zechariah – Elizabeth ❖ Joseph – Mary ❖ Zebedee – Salome ❖ Herod Antipas – Herodias ❖ Ananias – Sapphira

HOW THEY EARNED A LIVING

✶ *David* was a shepherd ✶ *Job* was a cattle and sheep farmer; he also owned many camels and donkeys ✶ *Nehemiah* was the cupbearer of King Artaxerxes ✶ *Amos* was a herdsman and a grower of figs ✶ *Peter, Andrew, James* and *John* were fishermen ✶ *Joseph* was a carpenter ✶ *Matthew* was a tax collector ✶ *Luke* was a doctor ✶ *Paul* was a tentmaker.

✶ In the 1903 translation of the Bible made by Ferrar Fentin, *Paul* and *Apollos* are described, rather oddly, in Acts 18:3 as 'landscape painters'.

Giants

Og, king of Bashan, was one of 'the remnant of the giants that dwelt at Ashtaroth and at Edrei' (Joshua 12:4). He had an iron (or possibly stone) bedstead nine cubits long and four cubits wide (= about 13 feet by 6 feet or 4 m by 2 m). ◆ Goliath was the giant Philistine soldier killed by David. His height is given (1 Samuel 17:4) as six cubits and a span (= about 9 to 10 feet or nearly 3 m). ◆ An Egyptian giant five cubits tall is mentioned at 1 Chronicles 11:23, and three other Philistine giants are spoken of at 1 Chronicles 20, one of whom had six fingers on each hand and six toes on each foot.

The Anakim and Emim, mentioned in Deuteronomy 2 and elsewhere, were also giants. The Anakim are named after Anak (Deuteronomy 9:2); 'Emim' means 'terrifying people'.

NAMES AND TITLES OF GOD

YAHWEH, YHWH

Strictly speaking, 'Yahweh' is the only name of God given in the Bible. All other terms are titles. This name is connected with a Hebrew verb meaning 'to be' and may mean 'I am' or 'he who is'. In many versions of the Bible, 'Yahweh' is translated as 'the Lord'. Since Hebrew words were originally written only with consonants, Yahweh may be written YHWH. It also appears in a shortened form 'Yah', especially in names (see page 35).

I AM

When God speaks to Moses out of the burning bush, and tells him to return to Egypt to lead the Israelites to freedom, Moses is worried that the Israelites will ask him the name of the god who has sent him:

> And God said unto Moses, I AM THAT I AM: and he said, Thus shalt thou say unto the children of Israel, I AM hath sent me unto you. This is my name for ever, and this is my memorial unto all generations. (Exodus 3:14–15)

YHWH is often referred to as the **Tetragrammaton,** which means 'a word of four letters' (from Greek *tetra* 'four' and *gramma* 'letter').

JEHOVAH

Because the name 'Yahweh' was considered too holy to pronounce, the word *adonay* (= 'my lord') was said in its place when the Hebrew Bible was being read. Eventually, the vowels of *adonay* were combined with the letters YHWH to give God a constructed name which was written as *Iehouah* in medieval Latin and which has become *Jehovah* in modern English.

EL = God

ELOHIM a word that is plural in form but used with a singular meaning; = God

ELOAH the singular form of ELOHIM; found most often in the Book of Job.

Deuteronomy 5:9 uses three of the names or titles for God:
I the Lord (YAHWEH) *your God* (ELOHIM) *am a jealous God* (EL).

EL is found in place names such as BETHEL, the 'house of God' and personal names such as ISHMAEL (see page 35).

EL ELYON = the most high God (Genesis 14:18)
EL OLAM = the everlasting God (Genesis 21:33)
EL SHADDAI = God Almighty (God the Mountain) (Exodus 6:3)

THE LORD OF HOSTS First used in the 1st Book of Samuel, it is the name of God used by David when challenging Goliath (1 Samuel 17:45). The 'hosts' may here have been the Israelite army, but soon came to mean the heavenly powers at God's command.

THE LORD GOD OF ISRAEL a term often used by the prophets

THE HOLY ONE OF ISRAEL used frequently in Isaiah, Jeremiah and the Psalms

THE MIGHTY ONE OF ISRAEL (Isaiah 1:24)

THE ANCIENT OF DAYS a title used in the Book of Daniel

ALPHA AND OMEGA (Revelation 1:8)

THE FATHER

OUR FATHER

The Holy Trinity

God the Father, God the Son and God the Holy Spirit; God in three Persons; the Triune God; the Great Three in One.

The word Trinity does not appear anywhere in the Bible. The word was first used to describe God by Tertullian (*c.* 155–220), a great North African Christian theologian.

SOME TITLES GIVEN TO JESUS

the Amen ✠ the Bread of Life ✠ the Christ ✠ the Dayspring ✠ the First and the Last ✠ the Good Shepherd ✠ the Great Shepherd of the sheep ✠ the Holy One and the Just ✠ the Holy One of God ✠ the Horn of Salvation ✠ Immanuel ✠ King of the Jews ✠ the King of Kings ✠ the Lamb of God ✠ the Last Adam ✠ the Light of the World ✠ the Lord ✠ our Lord ✠ the Man of Sorrows ✠ the Messiah ✠ our Passover ✠ the Prince of Peace ✠ the Redeemer ✠ the Saviour ✠ the Shepherd and Bishop of Souls ✠ the Son of David ✠ the Son of God ✠ the Son of Man ✠ the Son of the Blessed ✠ the Son of the Highest ✠ the True Vine ✠ the Word ✠ the Word of Life

SOME TITLES GIVEN TO THE HOLY SPIRIT

the Comforter ♦ the Holy Ghost ♦ the Paraclete ♦ the Spirit ♦ the Spirit of Christ ♦ the Spirit of God ♦ the Spirit of Life ♦ the Spirit of the Lord ♦ the Spirit of Truth; the spirit of wisdom and understanding, the spirit of counsel and might, the spirit of knowledge of the fear of the Lord (Isaiah 11)

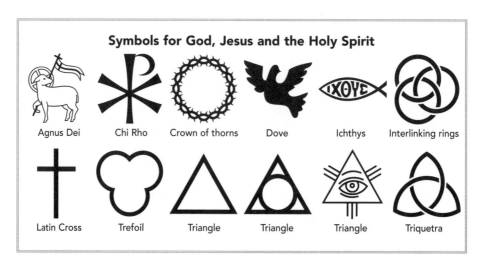

Symbols for God, Jesus and the Holy Spirit

| Agnus Dei | Chi Rho | Crown of thorns | Dove | Ichthys | Interlinking rings |
| Latin Cross | Trefoil | Triangle | Triangle | Triangle | Triquetra |

THE JEWISH CALENDAR

The traditional Jewish religious calendar is based on Year 1 being equivalent to 3761BC in the standard international Gregorian calendar. Unlike the Gregorian calendar, the Jewish calendar is based on movements of the moon; its months

therefore do not correspond exactly to the months of the solar Gregorian calendar, and the relationship between the months of the two calendars changes from year to year. Months in the Jewish calendar are 29 or 30 days long and begin with the new moon; the names are of Babylonian origin. Years are usually 12 months long, totalling 354 days (but 13 months in leap years or 'pregnant years'). The Jewish civil calendar has the same months as the religious calendar but begins at Tishri.

Month	Number	Length	Equivalent in the Gregorian calendar
NISSAN	1	30 days	March-April
IYAR or IYYAR	2	29 days	April-May
SIVAN	3	30 days	May-June
TAMMUZ	4	29 days	June-July
AV	5	30 days	July-August
ELUL	6	29 days	August-September
TISHRI	7	30 days	September-October
CHESHVAN	8	29 or 30 days	October-November
KISLEV	9	30 or 29 days	November-December
TEVET	10	29 days	December-January
SHEVAT	11	30 days	January-February
ADAR	12	29 days	February-March

In leap years, Adar is preceded by an extra month of 30 days, also named Adar. This extra Adar is known as Adar Aleph, Adar Rishon (= First Adar) or Adar I. The second Adar is then called Adar Bet, Adar Sheni (= Second Adar) or Adar II.

SABBATICAL YEARS

Just as every seventh day was for the Israelites a sabbath, a day of rest, so in accordance with the Law was every seventh year a sabbatical year, in which fields were left to lie fallow and vineyards and olive trees were left untended (Exodus 23, Leviticus 25). What grew by itself was not to be harvested but left for the poor, and what the poor did not take was left for animals. In order to provide food for the sabbatical year, God would ensure that in the sixth year the land would produce enough food for two years, and that there would be enough to last until the crops were harvested in the eighth year (Leviticus 25:21).

JUBILEES

Every fiftieth year was to be set apart as a jubilee year. In addition to the demands of the sabbatical year, all land that had been sold was returned to its previous owner or their heirs. (For this reason, Leviticus lays down that the price of land being sold must be based on the number of harvests before the next jubilee year, since what is actually being sold is not the land but the temporary use of the land.) Debts were cancelled and slaves were freed.

In Deuteronomy 15, it is laid down that debts were to be cancelled and slaves were to be freed every seventh year (i.e. in sabbatical years rather than only in jubilee years). Debts from non-Israelites, however, could be collected, and if slaves did not wish to leave their masters, they could opt to become slaves for life.

The word 'jubilee' comes from Hebrew *yobhel*, a ram's horn. The beginning of the jubilee year was marked by the blowing of a ram's-horn trumpet.

JEWISH RELIGIOUS FESTIVALS

THE FEAST OF UNLEAVENED BREAD or PASSOVER (in Hebrew, *Pesach*), celebrated to commemorate the Israelites' escape from Egypt, begins on 14 Nissan. Unleavened bread is eaten for seven days.

✡

THE FEAST OF HARVEST, also known as the FEAST OF WEEKS or THE DAY OF FIRST FRUITS (in Hebrew, *Shavuoth*), was a harvest festival but came to commemorate the giving of the Law to Moses at Sinai. It is celebrated on 6 Sivan. Since it occurs on the 50th day after the Passover, it is also known as Pentecost (Greek *pentekoste* 'fiftieth').

✡

THE FEAST OF INGATHERING (or FEAST OF TABERNACLES or FEAST OF BOOTHS, and in Hebrew, *Sukkoth*), is a thanksgiving festival held on 15–21 Tishri. Light

shelters or 'booths' are built to commemorate the huts or tents lived in by the Israelites in the Sinai desert after fleeing from Egypt.

✡

PURIM, THE FEAST OF LOTS, is celebrated on 14 or 15 Adar to commemorate the deliverance of the Persian Jews from a plot to have them massacred, as recounted in the Book of Esther.

✡

ROSH HASHANAH marks the Jewish New Year on 1 Tishri. 'Rosh Hashanah' means 'the head of the year'. During religious services, ram's-horn trumpets are blown.

✡

YOM KIPPUR, or the DAY OF ATONEMENT, on 10 Tishri is a day of prayer, fasting and repentance for sins.

✡

HANUKKAH, THE FEAST OF DEDICATION or FESTIVAL OF LIGHTS, is celebrated on 25–30 Kislev in memory of the capture and cleansing of the Temple by Judas Maccabaeus in 164 BC after its desecration by Antiochus Epiphanes. 'Hanukkah' is Hebrew for 'consecration'.

✡

9 AV is a day of prayer and fasting in memory of the destruction of Solomon's Temple by the Babylonians in 586BC and the Second Temple by the Romans in AD70.

ANGELS AND ARCHANGELS

The word 'angel' comes from Greek *anggelos*, meaning 'messenger'. Angels are God's messengers, though they have other functions. Archangels are chief angels (just as archbishops are chief bishops).

According to the 5th-century book *De Hierarchia Coelesti*, there are nine orders of angels, which the author divides into three groups of three. From highest to lowest, they are:

SERAPHIM, CHERUBIM and THRONES;
DOMINIONS, VIRTUES and POWERS;
PRINCIPALITIES, ARCHANGELS and ANGELS.

The only two angels named in the Old Testament are Gabriel and Michael. Both appear in the Book of Daniel. Gabriel explains the meaning of Daniel's visions (Daniel 8–9), while Michael is portrayed as the special guardian of Israel (Daniel 12:1). Other countries also have guardian angels.

In the New Testament, Gabriel announces to Zechariah the coming birth of John the Baptist (Luke 1:11–20), and tells Mary that she will give birth to Jesus (Luke 1:26–38). Michael is described in the Letter of Jude as 'contending with the devil about the body of Moses', and in Revelation 12 he and his angels fight against Satan and his angels (12:7).

In some non-biblical books, other angels and archangels are mentioned along with Gabriel and Michael. The names and numbers vary. For example, in the First Book of Enoch, the seven 'holy angels' are named as:

URIEL, *who is over the world and over Tartarus;*
RAPHAEL, *who is over the spirits of men;*
RAGUEL, *who takes vengeance on the world of the luminaries;*
MICHAEL, *who is set over the best part of mankind and over chaos;*
SARAQAEL, *who is set over the spirits, who sin in the spirit;*
GABRIEL, *who is over Paradise and the serpents and the Cherubim;*
REMIEL, *whom God set over those who rise.*

The angel Raphael appears in the story of Tobit (see page 152). Other names given to these angels include Sariel and Jeremiel.

Seraphim and cherubim

The only Bible reference to seraphim is Isaiah 6:1–7. Seraphim have six wings: two covering their faces, two covering their feet, and two for flying. Cherubim are generally represented as winged beings with feet and hands. In Ezekiel 10, cherubim are described as having four faces and four wings; in Ezekiel 41, the carved likenesses of cherubim are described as having two faces, one the face of a man and the other the face of a young lion. There were likenesses of cherubim on the Ark of the Covenant and also among the decorations of King Solomon's temple.

After the Fall, God placed cherubim and a flaming sword on the east side of the Garden of Eden to prevent Adam and Eve coming back into the garden and reaching the 'tree of life'.

SATAN

The devil and his rebellious angels are mentioned in Matthew 25:41, 2 Peter 2:4 and Jude 6.

BIBLICAL NAMES FOR THE DEVIL INCLUDE:

Satan ⚹ Lucifer ⚹ Beelzebub ⚹ Belial ⚹accuser ⚹ adversary ⚹ deceiver ⚹ liar ⚹ the prince of darkness ⚹ the prince of this world ⚹ the prince of the power of the air ⚹ the angel of the bottomless pit ⚹ the god of this world

Satan means 'adversary' ⚹ *Lucifer* means 'bringer of light' ⚹ *Beelzebub* means 'Lord of flies'.
The meaning of *Belial* is not certain, but it probably means 'worthlessness'.

STRANGE GODS

FOREIGN GODS MENTIONED IN THE BIBLE

✻ **ASHERAH** *a Canaanite mother-goddess; also her idol or a grove of trees planted in her honour.*

✻ **ASHTORETH** *a goddess of Sidon in Phoenicia and of the Philistines; a mother-goddess, also a goddess of fertility, love and war. Ashtaroth is the plural form of the name. In Greek she is called Astarte; in Assyrian Ishtar. She may be the 'queen of heaven' referred to in Jeremiah 44:17.*

✻ **BAAL** *Baal means 'lord', 'owner' or 'husband'. There were many Baals (or Baalim), but the chief Baal was a Canaanite and Phoenician god of storms and fertility. Baal-berith (= 'Lord of the covenant') was worshipped at Shechem (Judges 8:33). Baal-zebub (= 'Lord of flies') was the god of the Philistine city of Ekron (2 Kings 1); the name is probably a mocking corruption of 'Baal-zebul' (= 'Baal the Prince'). In the New Testament Beelzebub is considered the prince of demons.*

✻ **BEL** *the title given to the chief Babylonian god Marduk; the word is related to Baal*

✻ **CHEMOSH** *the god of the Moabites (1 Kings 11:7); children were sacrificed to him as burnt offerings.*

✻ **DAGON** *the principal god of the Philistines; a god of agriculture, often wrongly thought to be represented with the body of a fish.*

✻ **DIANA** *a Roman and Greek goddess of hunting and childbirth (in Greek, Artemis), and the chief goddess of Ephesus; her temple*

at Ephesus was one of the wonders of the ancient world.

✻ **MALCHAM, MILCOM, MOLECH, MOLOCH** *an Ammonite deity worshipped by human sacrifice.*

✻ **NEBO** *the Babylonian deity Nabu, son of Marduk; a god of science, learning and writing.*

✻ **NISROCH** *an Assyrian god.*

✻ **RIMMON** *a Syrian god.*

✻ **TAMMUZ** *a god corresponding to the Sumerian god Dumuzi, whose death was mourned by worshippers.*

Other foreign gods are **ADRAMMELECH, ANAMMELECH, ASHIMA, NERGAL, NIBHAZ, SUCCOTH-BENOTH** and **TARTAK** (2 Kings 17:30–31). **NERGAL** was the Babylonian god of destruction.

ANIMALS AND BIRDS OF THE BIBLE

■ Animals and birds are mentioned about 3,000 times in the Bible. Cattle are mentioned over 450 times, sheep about 400 times, horses, donkeys and lions about 140 times, camels over 60 times, pigs 20 times, and wolves 12 times.

■ There are 12 Hebrew words for sheep in the Bible, and ten words for cattle.

■ Before misfortune befell him, Job owned 7,000 sheep, 3,000 camels, 500 pairs of oxen and 500 she-asses. When his fortunes were restored, he owned twice as many.

■ The first mention of horses is in Genesis 47:17. The Israelite kings were banned from keeping large numbers of horses (Deuteronomy 17:16), but Solomon had 4,000 horses (2 Chronicles 9:25), or perhaps as many as 40,000 (1 Kings 4:26).

SHEEP AND GOATS

✦ Separating the sheep from the goats (Mathew 25:32): local breeds of sheep and goats were very similar in shape and colour and were often kept in flocks together. It was therefore quite a difficult task to separate them.

✦ Laban is the first person recorded in the Bible as having shorn sheep (Genesis 31:19). In the Laws set down in Leviticus, mixing wool and linen to make cloth was forbidden (19.19).

✦ Water-bottles were made out of goatskins. The head and legs of the goat were cut off, and the skin was removed in one piece. The skin was sewn up with the hair on the outside, leaving the neck open

to form the mouth of the bottle. The skin was then cured.

✦ The prohibition against boiling a kid in its mother's milk (Exodus 23.19) is due to this being a Canaanite fertility ceremony.

✦ A kid was the usual meal prepared for a guest or any small feast. Fatted calves were for more important occasions.

✦ The Bible records three cases of people being killed by lions: a prophet who disobeyed God's instructions (1 Kings 13), a man who refused a prophet's request (1 Kings 20) and the inhabitants of Samaria (2 Kings 17). Samson based a riddle on his finding a bees' nest with honey in the body of a lion he had killed: 'Out of the eater came forth meat, and out of the strong came forth sweetness' (Judges 14:14).

✦ There is only one example in the Bible of people being killed by bears: the children who made fun of Elijah (2 Kings 2: 24).

✦ Elephants are not mentioned in the Old or New Testaments, although ivory is mentioned 13 times. Thirty-two battle elephants feature in the First Book of Maccabees, in the Apocrypha, each carrying a wooden tower holding, it is said, 32 soldiers. Elephants were used as shock forces to disrupt the enemy. According to the account in Maccabees, the elephants were 'shown the blood of grapes and mulberries' to provoke them to fight (1 Maccabees 6:34).

✦ Just like people, animals such as donkeys and oxen were allowed to rest on the Sabbath (Exodus 23:12).

✦ Domestic cats are not mentioned in the Old or New Testaments, probably because they were not known in Palestine until Roman times. (The 'cats' in Baruch 6:22 is thought by many to refer to wild cats.) Dogs are mentioned but are generally considered unclean. However, in the Book of Tobit in the Apocrypha, Tobit's son Tobias has a pet dog.

✦ Unicorns are mentioned 12 times in the Old Testament, but since there are references to the 'horns' of a unicorn (e.g. Deuteronomy 33:17), it cannot mean the single-horned unicorn of fairy stories. It is generally accepted that the biblical unicorn is the aurochs, a wild ox that is the ancestor of domestic cattle.

LEVIATHAN AND BEHEMOTH

The leviathan (Hebrew *liwyathan*) mentioned in Job 41 may be a crocodile; at Psalm 104:26 it is a sea creature, possibly a whale or dolphin. Elsewhere it is used figuratively, e.g. representing Assyria and Babylonia in Isaiah 27. Behemoth (Job 40:15) is probably the hippopotamus, or perhaps the elephant.

Of the 400 or more birds that are resident in the Holy Land or pass through on migration, about 40 are mentioned in the Bible. Bats are included among birds in Leviticus 11:19.

Discounts for buying in quantity

According to Matthew 10:29, two sparrows cost a farthing. But according to Luke 12:6, you could get five sparrows for two farthings!

❖ The Hebrew words for 'fish' denoted not only fish but also shellfish, crustaceans and even some water animals such as seals.

❖ The word 'insect' is not used in early English translations of the Bible, including the KJV, because it only came into use in English in 1601.

❖ Locusts are mentioned 56 times in the Bible (more often than all other references to insects).

❖ 'Straining at a gnat' (Matthew 23.24) is more correctly 'straining out a gnat'. What Jesus is referring to is the practice of straining liquid before drinking it, or else drinking through a piece of cloth, in order to avoid inadvertently eating small insects, which were considered unclean. Camels were also considered unclean. So Jesus is accusing the scribes and Pharisees of being scrupulous about small matters such as tithes and ignoring the important things such as justice and mercy.

ANIMALS THAT MAY BE OR MUST NOT BE EATEN
(Leviticus 11 and Deuteronomy 14)

- Animals that can be eaten are those that chew the cud and have cloven hooves: the ox, the sheep, the goat, the hart, the roebuck, the fallow deer, the wild goat, the pygarg, the wild ox and the chamois.

- Animals that cannot be eaten are the camel, the hare and the coney (because they chew the cud but do not have cloven hooves), and swine (because they have cloven hooves but do not chew the cud). Also considered unclean are the weasel, the mouse, the tortoise, the ferret, the chameleon, the lizard, the snail and the mole.

- Of water creatures, only those that have fins and scales can be eaten.

- Birds that are not to be eaten are the eagle, the ossifrage, the ospray, the glede, the kite and the vulture; every raven after his kind; the owl, the night hawk, the cuckow, and the hawk; the little owl, the great owl, the swan, the pelican, the gier eagle, the cormorant, the stork, and the heron; the lapwing and the bat. Other birds can be eaten.

- 'Creeping things that fly' must not be eaten, except those that 'have legs above their feet' and jump: the locust, the bald locust, the beetle and the grasshopper.

It is not always certain what animals, birds or insects are denoted by the Hebrew names in these dietary laws. Compare Leviticus 11:30 in three versions of the Bible:

KING JAMES VERSION: *the ferret, the chameleon, the lizard, the snail and the mole*

REVISED STANDARD VERSION: *the gecko, the land crocodile, the lizard, the sand lizard and the chameleon*

NEW INTERNATIONAL VERSION: *the gecko, the monitor lizard, the wall lizard, the skink and the chameleon*

PLANTS OF THE BIBLE

● Cereals mentioned in the Bible, e.g. at Ezekiel 4:9, are wheat, barley, millet and 'fitches'. Fitches is a type of cereal known as spelt.

● In Isaiah 28:27, 'fitches' refers to a different plant, not a cereal but the nutmeg flower or black cumin, the seeds of which are used as a spice.

● Fruit trees and plants known in Bible times include grape vines, olive trees, fig trees, sycomore trees (a type of fig), date palms, pomegranate trees and apple trees.

● In Deuteronomy 20:19, the Israelites are forbidden to cut down fruit trees when besieging a city. They may eat the fruit, but they must leave the trees.

THE 'SEVEN SPECIES'

In Deuteronomy 8:8, Canaan is described as 'a land of wheat, and barley, and vines, and fig trees, and pomegranates; a land of olive oil and honey'. Honey may here refer to date syrup. These seven crops – wheat, barley, grapes, figs, pomegranates, olives and dates – are known as the 'seven species'.

The prophet Amos describes himself as a 'gatherer of sycomore fruit'. Zacchaeus the tax collector climbed up into a sycomore tree so that he could see Jesus above the heads of the crowd (Luke 19).

＊

The 'locusts' eaten by John the Baptist (Matthew 3:4) may have been the fruit of the carob tree. So also may have been the pods that the prodigal son fed to the swine (Luke 15:16).

＊

In Leviticus 23:40, the Israelites are instructed as part of the Feast of Tabernacles to take 'the boughs of goodly trees, branches of palm trees, and the boughs of thick trees, and willows of the brook'. The goodly trees are citron trees, the thick or leafy trees are myrtles. These four trees are known as the 'four species'.

✳

Nuts are mentioned twice in the Bible: at Genesis 43:11, the Hebrew word refers to pistachio nuts, while at Song of Solomon 6:11 the nuts are walnuts. The only other nut-like fruit mentioned in the Bible are almonds.

✳

Herbs and spices mentioned in the Bible include mint, cumin, coriander, dill ('anise' in the KJV), fitches (= black cumin), rue and saffron. In the Mishnah (see page 63), five plants are listed as suitable for the bitter herbs taken at the Passover; it is not absolutely certain what plants are intended, but they include lettuce and horseradish, and probably also chicory or endive.

✳

During the siege of Samaria described in 2 Kings 6:25, 'the fourth part of a cab of dove's dung' sold for five pieces of silver. (A 'cab' was about two pints.) 'Dove's dung' is not as bad as it sounds: it was a food plant of some sort, variously thought to have been the bulbs of the Star of Bethlehem, wild onions, or seed pods of some sort, perhaps carob beans.

✳

The burning bush out of which God spoke to Moses (Exodus 3) has been identified as either an acacia or the senna bush.

✳

The lilies of the field with which Jesus compares Solomon were not lilies but anemones. The tares that Jesus speaks of in his second parable of the sower (Matthew 13:24–30) are thought to be darnel, grasses that are common cornfield weeds.

✳

The plant that was used to make the crown of thorns with which Jesus was crowned by the Roman soldiers (Mark 15:17) may have been any of several thorny plants of the Middle East such as the Christ Thorn or the Thorny Burnet.

MORE BIBLE INFORMATION

WEIGHTS AND MEASURES IN THE BIBLE

Different versions of the Bible use different terms to translate the Hebrew words for weights and measures. The imperial and metric equivalents in the following tables are only approximate.

WEIGHT	gerah	= 0.05 shekel	= 0.02 oz, 0.6 g
	bekah	= 10 gerahs, 0.5 shekel	= 0.2 oz, 5.5 g
	shekel	= 2 bekahs	= 0.4 oz, 11.5 g
	mina, maneh	= 50 shekels	= 20 oz, 570 g
	talent	= 60 minas	= 75 lb, 34 kg
LENGTH	finger		= 0.75 in, 2 cm
	handbreadth	= 4 fingers	= 3 in, 8 cm
	span	= 3 handbreadths	= 9 in, 22 cm
	cubit	= 2 spans	= 18 in, 45 m
DRY CAPACITY	cab		= 1 qt, 1.2 l
	omer	= 1.8 cabs	= 2 qts, 2.2 l
	seah (= 'measure')	= 3.3 omers	= 7 qts, 7.3 l
	ephah	= 3 seahs, 10 omers	= 21 qts, 22 l
	lethech (= 'half-homer')	= 5 ephahs	= 3 bushels, 110 l
	homer or cor	= 10 ephahs	= 6 bushels, 220 l
LIQUID MEASURE	log		= 0.6 pt, 0.3 l
	cab	= 4 logs	= 2.5 pts, 1.3 l
	hin	= 3 cabs	= 1 gal, 4 l
	bath	= 6 hins	= 6 gals, 23 l
	cor	= 10 baths	= 61 gals, 230 l

MONEY

The first allusion to coins in the Bible is Haggai 1:6: 'He that earneth wages earneth wages to put it into a bag with holes.'

English terms
DRAM = daric
FARTHING = assarion; also = quadrans
MITE = lepton
PENNY = denarius
PIECE OF SILVER = drachma
POUND = mina

Hebrew terms
SHEKEL = 1 stater; = 4 drachmas or 4 denarii
MINA = 50 shekels; = 100 drachmas
TALENT = 60 minas; = 6,000 drachmas

Persian, Greek and Roman coins
AS a Roman copper coin; = 1/16 denarius
ASSARION a Greek copper coin; = 1 as
DARIC a Persian gold coin; = 4 drachmas
DRACHMA a Greek silver coin approx. = to the Roman denarius
DENARIUS a Roman silver coin; a day's wages for a labourer; the Good Samaritan paid the innkeeper 2 denarii to look after the injured man
LEPTON a Greek coin; the smallest unit of currency in the New Testament; = 1/2 quadrans
QUADRANS a Roman coin; = 1/4 as
STATER a Greek coin; = 4 drachmas

GEMS IN THE HIGH PRIEST'S BREASTPLATE

And thou shalt set in it four rows of stones: the first row shall be a sardius, a topaz, and a carbuncle. And the second row shall be an emerald, a sapphire, and a diamond. And the third row a ligure, an agate, and an amethyst. And the fourth row a beryl, and an onyx, and a jasper... (Exodus 28:17–20)

Scholars differ as to what precious stones are denoted by these terms:
✱ THE NEW INTERNATIONAL VERSION lists them as ruby, topaz, beryl, turquoise, sapphire, emerald, jacinth, agate, amethyst, chrysolite, onyx and jasper
✱ THE GOOD NEWS BIBLE has ruby, topaz, garnet, emerald, sapphire, diamond, turquoise, agate, amethyst, beryl, carnelian and jasper.

MUSICAL INSTRUMENTS IN THE BIBLE

In Genesis 4:21, Jubal is described as the ancestor of musicians who play the harp and organ. ✱ In 1 Samuel 10:5, Samuel tells Saul that he will meet prophets playing a psaltery, a tabret, a pipe and a harp. ✱ In 2 Samuel 6:5 David and the Israelites play 'instruments made of fir wood, even on harps, and on psalteries, and on timbrels, and on cornets, and on cymbals'. ✱ In Daniel 3, the Babylonians are commanded to bow down and worship Nebuchadnezzar's golden idol when they hear the sound of 'the cornet, flute, harp, sackbut, psaltery and dulcimer'.

●STRINGED INSTRUMENTS: *harp, psaltery, viol (probably a type of harp or lyre); what the KJV calls a 'sackbut' (an old wind instrument) was probably a harp or lyre.*

●WIND INSTRUMENTS: *cornet, trumpet, flute, pipe; a 'dulcimer' was not the stringed instrument played today but probably a form of pipe or bagpipes; the 'organ' was probably also a type of pipes.*

●PERCUSSION INSTRUMENTS: *timbrel and tabret (like tambourines); cymbals and bells; the cornets of 2 Samuel 6:5 were percussion instruments, possibly castanets or sistrums (an instrument that is shaken and rattled)*

●*The shofar or ram's-horn trumpet had both religious and military uses. Shofars were played at the conquest of Jericho (see page 114). The shofar is now played in the synagogue at Yom Kippur and Rosh Hashanah (see page 45). Not all shofars are made of rams' horns; other animals' horns are permitted, such as the ibex or kudu (a type of antelope).*

Stars and constellations

Three constellations are mentioned in the Bible, mostly in the Book of Job: Arcturus (Job 9:9 – actually the Great Bear), Orion and the Pleiades. In addition, Mazzaroth (Job 38:32) may be the Great Bear and the Little Bear, or it may denote the signs of the zodiac. The 'chambers of the south' (Job 9:9) may be southern stars or constellations.

SOME BIBLE 'FIRSTS'

* first man – ADAM
* first woman – EVE
* first child – CAIN
* first twins – ESAU AND JACOB
* first concubine – HAGAR
* first death – ABEL
* first murder – CAIN AND ABEL
* first suicide – SAMSON (OR SAUL, IF YOU DON'T COUNT SAMSON'S DEATH AS SUICIDE)
* first person not to die – ENOCH
* first prophet – ENOCH (SEE JUDE 14)
* first surgical operation – GOD REMOVING ONE OF ADAM'S RIBS
* first clothes – APRONS OF FIG LEAVES
* first musical instruments – HARP AND ORGAN
* first city – ENOCH (BUILT BY CAIN)
* first boat – THE ARK
* first covenant – BETWEEN GOD AND NOAH
* first person to get drunk – NOAH
* first person to be imprisoned – JOSEPH
* first kiss – ISAAC AND JACOB
* first person to laugh – ABRAHAM
* first person to weep – HAGAR
* first city captured in Canaan – JERICHO
* first king mentioned in Old Testament – MELCHIZEDEK, KING OF SALEM (THOUGH THE EGYPTIAN PHARAOH IS MENTIONED EARLIER)
* first king of Israel – SAUL
* first disciples of Jesus – PETER AND ANDREW
* first miracle by Jesus – TURNING WATER INTO WINE AT CANA
* first Christian martyr – STEPHEN

SOME HEBREW WORDS

AMEN: = 'surely' or 'certainly' in Hebrew; when Jesus says 'verily', this translates the word 'amen'.

♦

HALLELUJAH: = 'Praise Yah(weh)'; the Greek and Latin form used in the New Testament is 'alleluia'.

♦

HOSANNA: = the Greek form of a Hebrew phrase meaning 'please save us'; the cry of the crowds as Jesus entered Jerusalem (Matthew 21:9) echoes Psalm 118:25–26.

♦

MESSIAH: = 'anointed' in Hebrew and Aramaic; the Greek equivalent is 'christos'.

♦

SHIBBOLETH: = 'flowing stream' or 'ear of corn'; in Judges 12, the Ephraimites give themselves away by pronouncing the word 'sibboleth'.

SOME ENGLISH EXPRESSIONS OF BIBLICAL ORIGIN

forbidden fruit (Genesis 2:17)

✳

my brother's keeper (Genesis 4:9)

✳

the mark of Cain (Genesis 4:15)

✳

a mess of pottage (Genesis 25:34)

✳

an eye for an eye (Exodus 21:24)

✳

the apple of one's eye (Deuteronomy 32:10)

✳

a man after one's own heart (1 Samuel 13:14)

✳

lick the dust (Psalm 72:9)

✳

at one's wits' end (Psalm 107:27)

✳

escape by the skin of one's teeth (Job 19:20)

✳

gird one's loins (Job 38:3)

✳

have feet of clay (Daniel 2:33)

✳

the writing on the wall (Daniel 5:24)

the lions' den (Daniel 6:16)

✳

go the second mile (Matthew 5:41)

✳

cast pearls before swine (Matthew 7:6)

✳

the straight and narrow (Matthew 7:14 – actually 'strait', not 'straight')

✳

wolves in sheep's clothing (Matthew 7:15)

✳

a den of thieves (Matthew 21:13)

✳

the sheep and the goats (Matthew 25:32)

✳

die the death (Mark 7:10)

✳

a good samaritan (Luke 10:33)

✳

the prodigal son (Luke 15)

✳

a thorn in the flesh (2 Corinthians 12:7)

✳

a multitude of sins (James 5:20 and 1 Peter 4:8)

Bible names in American diner slang

Adam 'n' Eve = two poached eggs ✦ *Adam and Eve on a raft* = poached eggs on toast ✦ *Adam and Eve on a raft, and wreck 'em*: scrambled eggs on toast ✦ *Eve with a lid on* = apple pie ✦ *Eve with a mouldy lid* = apple pie with slice of cheese ✦ *First Lady* = spareribs (Eve was formed out of Adam's rib) ✦ *Noah's boy* = ham (Ham was one of Noah's three sons) ✦ *Noah's boy on bread* = a ham sandwich

... and a British pud

Eve's pudding = a British pudding of apples covered in sponge cake

SIGNIFICANT BIBLE NUMBERS

1
* 'Hear, O Israel: The Lord our God is one Lord' (Deuteronomy 6:4)
* Jesus said, 'I and my Father are one' (John 10:30)
* In marriage, two people become 'one flesh' (Matthew 19:6)

2
* The animals entered the Ark in twos
* The Ten Commandments were written on two stone tablets
* Two was the minimum number of witnesses required in an accusation (Deuteronomy 19:15)

3
* Noah had three sons
* Abraham was visited by three men (Genesis 18)
* David had to choose between three years of famine, three months of defeat or three days of disease (1 Chronicles 21:12)
* Jonah spent three days and nights

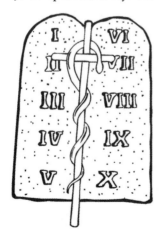

in the belly of the fish
* There were three different gifts brought by the Magi
* There were three crosses at Calvary
* Jesus rose on the third day
* Paul lists three special virtues – faith, hope and charity (love)
* There are three Persons in the Trinity (though this word does not appear in the Bible)

4
* There are four letters in God's name YHWH
* The river that flowed out of Eden split into four
* The power of God is shown by four winds from the four quarters of heaven (Jeremiah 49:36)
* Ezekiel saw four living creatures (1:5)
* Daniel had a vision of four great beasts rising out of the sea (7:3)
* There are four gospels
* John had a vision of the four horsemen of the Apocalypse (Revelation 6)
* There are four corners of the earth (Revelation 7:1)
* There will be four angels of destruction (Revelation 9:14)

5
* There are 'Five Books of Moses' (Genesis to Deuteronomy)

6 ✴ The universe was created in six days

7 ✴ God rested on the seventh day
✴ Every seventh day is a day of rest
✴ Every seventh year was a sabbatical year
✴ After seven times seven years, the next year was a Jubilee
✴ At Jericho, seven priests blew seven trumpets, and on the seventh day the Israelites marched round the city seven times (Joshua 6)
✴ We must forgive seventy times seven times
✴ Seven deacons were appointed in the early church
✴ John wrote to seven churches (Revelation 1:4)
✴ There are seven archangels

8 ✴ There were eight people in the Ark.

10 ✴ There were ten patriarchs before the Flood
✴ There were ten plagues in Egypt
✴ There are Ten Commandments
✴ 'Ten' is the number in many parables – ten talents, ten virgins, ten pieces of silver
✴ Paul lists ten powers that cannot separate us from the love of God (Romans 8:38–39)
✴ There are ten sins that prevent people inheriting the kingdom of God (1 Corinthians 6:9–10)
✴ John saw a dragon with ten horns (Revelation 12:3)

12 ✴ There are 12 months in the year, and 12 hours in the day (John 11:9)
✴ Jacob had 12 sons
✴ There were 12 tribes of Israel
✴ Jesus appointed 12 apostles
✴ There are 12 stars, 12 gates, 12 angels, 12 pearls, 12 fruit mentioned in Revelation

30 ✴ Judas was paid 30 pieces of silver

40 ✴ It rained for 40 days and nights during the Flood
✴ The Israelites spent 40 years in the wilderness
✴ Moses spent 40 days and nights on Mount Sinai
✴ Jesus spent 40 days in the wilderness

50 ✴ Every 50th year was a Jubilee

70 ✴ There were 70 people in Jacob's family (Genesis 46:27)
✴ 70 elders were appointed to help Moses (Numbers 11:16)
✴ The people of Judah spent 70 years in Babylon
✴ Jesus sent out 70 apostles (Luke 10:1)

666 ✴ see page 192

THE OLD TESTAMENT AND THE JEWISH BIBLE

THE OLD TESTAMENT

In the Christian Bible the 39 books of the Old Testament are often divided up as follows:

✝

THE BOOKS OF THE LAW
Genesis, Exodus, Leviticus, Numbers, Deuteronomy

These books are often referred to as the Pentateuch, meaning the 'Five Books' (from Greek *penta* 'five' and *teuchos* 'tool, book').

✝

THE HISTORICAL BOOKS
Joshua, Judges, Ruth, 1 Samuel, 2 Samuel, 1 Kings, 2 Kings, 1 Chronicles, 2 Chronicles, Ezra, Nehemiah, Esther

THE POETICAL AND PHILOSOPHICAL BOOKS
Job, Psalms, Proverbs, Ecclesiastes, Song of Solomon

✝

THE MAJOR PROPHETS
Isaiah, Jeremiah, Lamentations, Ezekiel, Daniel

✝

THE MINOR PROPHETS
Hosea, Joel, Amos, Obadiah, Jonah, Micah, Nahum, Habakkuk, Zephaniah, Haggai, Zechariah, Malachi

The term 'minor prophets' does not mean that they are of less importance than the 'major prophets', simply that their books are relatively short.

THE JEWISH BIBLE

The books of the Hebrew Bible are set out in a different order. The Bible is divided into three sections – the Law, the Prophets and the Writings (in Hebrew the *Torah*, the *Nebiim* and the *Kethubim*).

✿

The Hebrew Bible is sometimes called the Tanakh, from the initial letters of *Torah*, *Nebiim* and *Kethubim*.

THE LAW

As in the Christian Bible, the Law consists of the five books from Genesis to Deuteronomy.

The Prophets

The Prophets falls into two sections:

✿ The **Former Prophets** consists of Joshua, Judges, Samuel and Kings (the latter being generally treated as two books, not four as in the Christian Old Testament).

✿ The **Latter Prophets** are Isaiah, Jeremiah, Ezekiel and 'The Twelve'. The Twelve consists of the books from Hosea to Malachi; they are, however, traditionally thought of as a single book.

THE WRITINGS

❖ *The Writings consist of eleven books: Psalms, Proverbs, Job, Ecclesiastes, Song of Solomon, Ruth, Lamentations, Esther, Ezra–Nehemiah, Chronicles and Daniel.*

Notice that in the Jewish Bible, Daniel is not included among the Prophets.

❖ *Ezra + Nehemiah and 1 + 2 Chronicles form two books, not four, so the Jewish Bible consists of 24 books: five books of the Law, four books of Former Prophets and four of Latter Prophets, and eleven books of the Writings. It has sometimes been referred to as the 'Twenty-four Holy Scriptures'.*

❖ *In 2 Esdras, a book belonging to the Apocrypha (see next page), the story is told that Esdras the scribe (= the 'Ezra' of the Old Testament) dictated from memory the 24 books of Scripture, and 70 other books that he received from God. However, God instructed Ezra only to make the 24 books available for 'the worthy and unworthy' to read while keeping back the other 70 books for 'the wise'.*

❖ *Five books of the Writings – Ecclesiastes, Song of Solomon, Ruth, Lamentations, Esther – are known as the 'Five Scrolls'. They are each connected with and read at one of the five major Jewish festivals: Ecclesiastes at the Feast of Tabernacles, the Song of Solomon at the Passover, Ruth at the Feast of Weeks, Lamentations on the ninth day of Ab (a day of fasting in memory of the destruction of the Temple), and Esther at the Festival of Purim.*

The TALMUD is a code of Jewish civil and religious law, comprising the MISHNAH and the GEMARA. The Mishnah is a collection of commentaries on the Jewish Law set out in the Bible. The Gemara is a commentary on the Mishnah.

The Samaritan Bible consists solely of the five books from Genesis to Deuteronomy. *(Who are the Samaritans? See page 176.)*

THE 'EXTRA' BOOKS OF THE BIBLE

THE SEPTUAGINT

The Greek translation of the Jewish Bible known as the Septuagint (see page 15) included some books that were not in the Hebrew Bible. Among these are some additions to the Book of Esther, some further stories about Daniel, a book similar to Proverbs attributed to King Solomon, and some historical books. As the early Christian church used the Greek Old Testament, these books were accepted as part of the canon of the Bible.

A canon is a list of religious books accepted as scripture, from Greek *kanon* = 'measuring rod'.

ST JEROME

When St Jerome came to revise the Latin Bible to produce the version known as the Vulgate (see page 15), he felt he should reject from the Old Testament all books that were not in the Hebrew Bible. These other books he called 'apocrypha', meaning 'hidden writings'.

THE APOCRYPHA

The 14 books included in the Apocrypha are: 1 & 2 Esdras, Tobit, Judith, Additions to Esther, the Wisdom of Solomon, Ecclesiasticus (Sirach), Baruch (with the Epistle of Jeremiah), the Song of the Three Holy Children, the History of Susanna, Bel and the Dragon, the Prayer of Manasses, 1 and 2 Maccabees.

In these 14 books, there are 183 chapters, 6,031 verses, 125,185 words and 1,063,876 letters.

THE ROMAN CATHOLIC CHURCH

In spite of Jerome's views, the Roman Catholic Church accepted most of these books as 'deuterocanonical', meaning 'belonging to a secondary canon', and they have normally been included in Roman Catholic versions of the Bible, interspersed among the other books of the Old Testament. For example, Tobit and Judith follow Nehemiah, the Wisdom of Solomon and Ecclesiasticus follow the Song of Solomon, Baruch follows Lamentations, and 1 & 2 Maccabees follow Malachi.

Protestant churches have tended to reject the Apocrypha altogether, although they were formerly included in the King James Version, fitted in between the Old and New Testaments, and they are sometimes included in modern translations.

THE ORTHODOX CHURCH

The Orthodox Churches vary in the number of books they accept in their canons, but they include all the Apocrypha plus other books in addition. The Ethiopian Orthodox Church has the largest Bible of all, containing 81 books.

ENOCH

Among the books included in the canon of the Ethiopian Orthodox Church is one called 1 Enoch. It is supposedly written by the patriarch Enoch, the father of Methuselah (Genesis 5:21). Although this book is not included in the Bibles of most Christian denominations, it is quoted in the Letter of Jude (verse 14).

THE BOOKS OF JASHER, SAMUEL, IDDO AND OTHERS

Several books are mentioned in the Old Testament but not included in it. Among these are:

the book of Jasher (Joshua 10:13, 2 Samuel 1:18) ✷ *the book of the acts of Solomon* (1 Kings 11:41) ✷ *the books of Samuel the seer, Nathan the prophet and Gad the seer* (1 Chronicles 29:29) ✷ *the book of Shemaiah the prophet and Iddo the seer* (2 Chronicles 12:15) ✷ *the book in which Samuel set down the nature of a kingdom* (1 Samuel 10:25) ✷ *the books of the chronicles of the kings of Israel* (1 Kings 14:19) *and of the kings of Judah* (1 Kings 14:29) ✷ *the book of the kings of Israel and Judah* (1 Chronicles 9:1), *the book of the kings of Judah and Israel* (2 Chronicles 16:11), *and the story of the book of the kings* (2 Chronicles 24:27).

... AND OTHER BOOKS NOT INCLUDED IN BIBLES

The early Christian church also produced books that were not accepted into the New Testament. These included apocryphal gospels supposedly describing Jesus' childhood and apocryphal Acts of apostles such as Peter, Andrew, John, Thomas and Paul, often enlarging (in sometimes not very credible ways) on events recorded in the biblical Acts of the Apostles and recording the apostles' martyrdoms.

THE OLD TESTAMENT

The Old Testament, the Hebrew Bible, describes the history of the Jewish people from the creation of the world up to the second half of the 5th century BC. But the Old Testament is not just a history book, it is a book of history written specifically from a religious perspective. It is not just the history of a people, but the history of a people who see themselves as having a unique relationship with God and a unique calling from God. That relationship and that calling – and the repeated failure of God's people to live up to them – are the threads that run through and link in some way or another almost all the books of the Hebrew Bible.

The Old Testament does not, however, consist solely of history. In its books you find also poetry, philosophy, prophecy and, depending on your understanding of certain passages such as the early chapters of Genesis or the book ascribed to the prophet Jonah, perhaps also myths and parables.

The Five Books of Moses

The first five books in the Old Testament are the Books of Moses or the Books of the Law: Genesis, Exodus, Leviticus, Numbers and Deuteronomy. In them are told the story of creation, of Adam and Eve, of Noah, Abraham and the early patriarchs, of the flight from Egypt, the receiving of the Law at Sinai, the 40 years in the wilderness, and the Israelites' arrival at the borders of Canaan. We read of covenants made between God and Noah, Abraham and Moses. From Exodus to Deuteronomy, Moses is the key character, and Deuteronomy ends with his death within sight of Canaan.

THE HISTORY BOOKS

The five Books of Moses are followed by two sets of history books. One set consists of the books of Joshua, Judges, 1 & 2 Samuel and 1 & 2 Kings, and covers the period from the conquest of Canaan by the Israelites to the conquest of Judah and Jerusalem by the Babylonians. The other set consists of 1 & 2 Chronicles, Ezra and Nehemiah: it begins with Adam and continues through to the return of the Jews from Babylon and the rebuilding of the Temple and the walls of Jerusalem. Included with these histories are the stories of Ruth (the great-grandmother of King David) and Esther (a Jewish girl who became a queen of Persia).

THE POETIC AND PHILOSOPHICAL BOOKS

The next five books of the Old Testament are Job (a philosophical consideration of the problem of suffering and justice), the Psalms, the Proverbs (a collection of moral and religious teachings), Ecclesiastes (a philosophical study of the meaning of life), and the Song of Songs (a book of love poetry). Another poetical book, Lamentations, consisting of five poems lamenting the destruction of Jerusalem by the Babylonians, follows the Book of Jeremiah.

The prophetic books

The remaining 16 books are the books of the prophets from Isaiah to Malachi. These are not in historical order. Chronologically, the earliest prophets are Joel and Amos, not Isaiah and Jeremiah. There is a question whether Jonah and Daniel are truly prophetic books at all, but on the other hand, Daniel is for many people an important prophet. Among the major themes to be found in the books of the prophets are God's love, mercy, justice and holiness; his judgement on Israel for its moral and religious failings; and the hope of a better future with the coming of God's Messiah. Old Testament prophecy ends with Zechariah and Malachi.

OLD TESTAMENT TIMELINE

Some of the early dates in this timeline are uncertain. Dates before Abraham are even more problematical, and are not included here. Tables of dates of the kings of Judah and Israel, the prophets, and the kings of Assyria, Babylon and Persia are to be found on pages 136, 141 and 139.

Year BC	Biblical events
C. 2000–1800	Abraham probably lived during this period, but possibly even earlier and possibly slightly later
C.1750–1650	Joseph probably lived during this period. According to Exodus 12:40, the Hebrews were in Egypt for 430 years (but according to Paul in his letter to the Galatians, following the text of the Septuagint, it was 430 years from Abraham to the covenant at Sinai after the Exodus)
C.1350–1250	Moses
C.1290	The Exodus from Egypt (Some scholars would place this at an earlier date, c.1440BC; the life of Moses and the conquest of Canaan would therefore also have to be placed earlier.)
MID-13TH – MID-11TH CENTURIES	Conquest of Canaan; Joshua and Judges
C.1050–1010	Saul king of Israel
1010–970	David king of Israel
970–930	Solomon king of Israel
966–959	Solomon builds the first Temple; begun in the fourth year of his reign and completed in the eleventh year

930	The kingdom of Israel splits into a northern kingdom (Israel) and a southern kingdom (Judah)
722	The fall of the northern kingdom to the Assyrians
621	Discovery of the Book of the Law (Deuteronomy)
609	Assyria falls to the Babylonians
597	Jerusalem surrendered to the Babylonians
586	The fall of Judah to the Babylonians; Jerusalem and the Temple are destroyed
539	Babylon falls to the Persians
538	Cyrus allows some Jews to return to Jerusalem to rebuild the Temple
516	The Second Temple is completed
445	Nehemiah travels to Jerusalem; the city walls are rebuilt.

Old Testament history can be roughly divided into five epochs:
the patriarchs ■ Egypt ■ the judges ■ the kings ■ the exile and the return.

THE FIVE BOOKS OF MOSES

The first five books of the Bible are Genesis, Exodus, Leviticus, Numbers and Deuteronomy. Traditionally ascribed to Moses, though no such claim is made in the books themselves, they are collectively known as the 'Five Books of Moses'. Whatever part Moses had in the writing of these books, he cannot have written the very last section of Deuteronomy – chapter 34, verses 5 to 12 – which records his death and burial.

The Pentateuch

These five books are also known as the Pentateuch, from Greek *penta* 'five' and *teuchos* 'tool, book'.

The first six books of the Bible, i.e. the Pentateuch + the Book of Joshua, are sometimes referred to as the Hexateuch (from Greek *hexa* 'six').

THE ENGLISH AND HEBREW NAMES OF THE BOOKS

English name Meaning and origin

GENESIS	*Creation; 'Genesis' was the title given to the book in the Greek translation of the Jewish Bible known as the Septuagint*
EXODUS	*Going out; via Latin, from Greek* ex *'out'* + hodos *'a way'*
LEVITICUS	*From Latin* Leviticus (liber) *'(the book) of the Levites'*
NUMBERS	Arithmoi *'numbers' was the title given to the book in the Septuagint; there are two censuses and several lists of tribal numbers in the book*
DEUTERONOMY	*Second law, i.e. a second copy of the Law; from Greek* deuteros *'second'* + nomos *'law'*

The Hebrew names for these books are taken from words at or close to the beginning of each book:

English name	Hebrew name	Meaning
GENESIS	BERESHIT	*In the beginning*
EXODUS	SHEMOT	*Names*
LEVITICUS	WAYYIQRA'	*And he called*
NUMBERS	BEMIDBAR	*In the desert*
DEUTERONOMY	DEVARIM	*Words*

THE CONTENTS OF THE BOOKS

GENESIS

Genesis begins with the Creation and the story of Adam and Eve. Following this are the stories of Noah and the Flood, and of the attempt to build the Tower of Babel. Then there are the lives of the patriarchs: Abraham, Isaac, Jacob and Joseph, whose family settles in Egypt.

EXODUS

Now seen by the Egyptians as a threat, the Israelites are reduced virtually to the status of slaves. God commissions Moses to lead the Israelites to freedom. After the Egyptians suffer ten plagues, the Pharaoh allows the Israelites to leave Egypt. At Sinai, God delivers the Ten Commandments to Moses. Many other laws are written in Exodus.

LEVITICUS

This book is concerned with religious and moral duties and laws.

In Leviticus 19:18 is written for the first time a key teaching in the Bible:

Thou shalt love thy neighbour as thyself.

NUMBERS

As well as lists of tribal numbers, this book continues the story of the Israelites' journey to Canaan. Spies sent into Canaan to assess the situation come back with a false story of the size and power of

the enemies the Israelites would have to face there. Disheartened, the Israelites want to return to Egypt. God punishes their rebellion by condemning them to 40 years in the wilderness before entering the Promised Land.

DEUTERONOMY

Deuteronomy is about renewal of the covenant. Although part of the Pentateuch, it runs parallel to the previous four. Moses again dictates to the Israelites the laws set out in Exodus, Leviticus and Numbers.

In Deuteronomy 6:4–5, another key biblical teaching is set out:

Hear, O Israel, the Lord our God is one Lord: And thou shalt love the Lord thy God with all thine heart, and with all thy soul, and with all thy might.

THE CREATION STORIES

There are two creation stories in the Bible, in the first two chapters of the Book of Genesis. They are not easily reconciled, as the order of what was created when differs in the two books.

THE FIRST CREATION STORY:
GOD CREATES THE WORLD IN SIX DAYS

In the beginning God created the heaven and the earth.

THE FIRST DAY: *GOD CREATES LIGHT*

In the beginning the earth was unformed and empty; and there was darkness. And God said, Let there be light: and there was light. And God divided the light from the darkness. God called the light Day, and the darkness Night.

THE SECOND DAY: *GOD CREATES THE SKY*

Then God said, Let there be a solid dome in the middle of the waters. And God made the dome, and separated the waters which were under the dome from the waters which were above it. And God called the dome Heaven.

THE THIRD DAY: *GOD CREATES LAND AND PLANTS*

God said, Let the water under heaven be gathered together, and let dry land appear. And God called the dry land Earth; and he called the water Sea. And the earth brought forth grass, and plants yielding seed, and trees producing fruit.

According to this version of the Creation story as recounted in 2 Esdras (a book of the Apocrypha), God gathered the water together into one seventh of the surface of the Earth while the other six sevenths became land (2 Esdras 6:42).

THE FOURTH DAY: *GOD CREATES THE SUN, MOON AND STARS*

Then God said, Let there be lights in the sky to separate the day from the night; and let them indicate the seasons, and the days and years. And let them shine light on the earth. And God made two great lights: he made a larger light to govern the day, and a smaller light to govern the night. He also made the stars. And God set them in the dome of heaven to shine light upon the earth, and to govern the day and night, and to separate the light from the darkness.

THE FIFTH DAY: *GOD CREATES SEA CREATURES AND BIRDS*

Then God said, Let the waters produce many living creatures, and let the air be filled with birds. And God created all sorts of sea creatures, large and small, and all sorts of birds.

THE SIXTH DAY: *GOD CREATES LAND ANIMALS AND HUMAN BEINGS*

On the sixth day, God made many sorts of animals – wild animals and domestic animals, large animals and small creeping and scurrying animals. And then God created human beings. He created them in his own image, both male and female. They were to rule over all the animals God had created.

THE SEVENTH DAY: *GOD RESTS*

On the seventh day God had finished his work, and he rested.

A 6000-YEAR-OLD UNIVERSE?

James Ussher (1581–1656) was an Irish Anglican archbishop, now mostly remembered for his placing the date and time of the Creation at noon on 23 October, 4004 BC.

A very learned man and a great scholar, Ussher based his calculations on dates and ages given in the Bible, and by correlating the dates of biblical events with those given in the histories of other cultures such as the Babylonians.

Nowadays Ussher is frequently mocked for the Bible-based assumptions behind his calculations, but Harvard scientist Stephen Jay Gould has described Ussher's work as 'an honorable effort' that represents 'the best of scholarship in his time'.

Other scholars around the same period came up with very similar dates. For example, the Dutch historian Joseph Scaliger (1540–1609), one of the greatest intellectuals of his day, calculated the year of Creation to be 3950 BC.

The traditional Jewish calendar is based on the date of Creation being October 3761BC.

SOME THOUGHTS ON THE CREATION

That the universe was formed by a fortuitous concourse of atoms, I will no more believe than that the accidental jumbling of the alphabet would fall into a most ingenious treatise of philosophy.
Jonathan Swift (1667–1745), English writer

✳

Posterity will some day laugh at the foolishness of modern materialistic philosophy. The more I study nature, the more I am amazed at the Creator.
Louis Pasteur (1822–95), French scientist

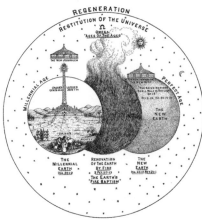

But on the other hand ...

Had I been present at the Creation, I would have given some useful hints for the better ordering of the universe.
Alfonso the Wise (1221–84), King of Castile (Spain)

✳

Man was made at the end of the week's work, when God was tired.
Mark Twain (1835–1910), American writer

THE SECOND CREATION STORY:
GOD CREATES THE FIRST HUMAN BEINGS

While in the first Creation story, human beings are the last creatures to be created, in this story God begins with the creation of a man and finishes with the creation of a woman to be his companion.

GOD CREATES ADAM:

> God formed the man out of the dust of the ground, and breathed into his nostrils the breath of life; and the man became a living being.

GOD CREATES THE GARDEN IN EDEN:

> Then God created a garden in Eden, and he made all kinds of tree grow that were pleasant to look at and good for food. He also planted the tree of life and the tree of knowledge of good and evil in the middle of the garden. And God put the man into the garden of Eden to work in it and to look after it.

GOD CREATES ANIMALS:

> God said to himself, It is not good that the man should be alone, so I will make a suitable companion for him. And God created all sorts of animals and birds and brought them to Adam to see what he would call them. And Adam gave names to all the domestic animals and wild animals and to all the birds. But none of them was a suitable companion for him.

GOD CREATES EVE:

> So God caused Adam to fall asleep. Then he took out one of Adam's ribs. And from the rib, God had made a woman. God brought her to Adam, and Adam said, This is now bone from my bones, and flesh from my flesh: she will be called 'woman', because she was taken out of 'man'.

THE STORY THAT WASN'T TOLD IN THE BIBLE!

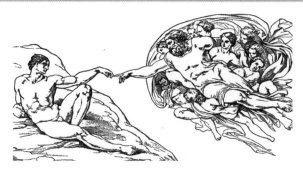

God could see that Adam was not entirely happy in the Garden of Eden, and asked him what was wrong. Adam said he was feeling lonely, because he didn't have anyone to talk to. So God told Adam he would create a companion for him.

God said: 'This person will gather food for you, cook for you, and wash your clothes for you. ('What are clothes?' asked Adam. 'We'll talk about that another day,' said God.) She will bear your children, but never ask you to get up in the middle of the night when they cry. She will always love you, she won't nag you, and she'll always agree with whatever you say.'
Adam liked the sound of this, and asked God, 'What will a companion like that cost?' 'An arm and a leg,' replied God. Adam thought for a moment, and then asked, 'Well, what could I get for just a rib?'

(There are many versions of this story. I apologize that I do not know who to attribute it to. G.D.)

ADAM'S FIRST WIFE

According to a non-biblical myth, Adam's first wife was not Eve, but Lilith. Lilith was banished from the Garden of Eden because she would not submit to Adam's authority. Then God created Eve. According to the myth, Lilith became a demon who stole and killed newborn babies.

❖ *The name 'Adam' means 'mankind'. It is used with this meaning about 500 times in the Old Testament. It sounds like the Hebrew word for 'ground'. Adam named his wife 'Eve' because she would be the mother of all living beings (the Hebrew form of 'Eve' being similar to a word that means 'living').*

---

helpmeet

The word 'helpmeet', meaning 'a helpful companion, a husband or wife', comes from a misreading of Genesis 2:18 in the King James Version of the Bible, where God says:

'It is not good that the man should be alone; I will make him an help meet for him', which means 'someone suitable to help him'.

The phrase 'help meet' came to be understood as a 'helpmeet', and later 'helpmate'.

❖ *Adam is also the name of a town mentioned in the Book of Joshua. The waters of the River Jordan piled up at Adam until the river-bed was dry further downstream, allowing the Israelites to cross the river into Canaan (Joshua 3).*

WHAT DID ADAM AND EVE NOT HAVE THAT ALL THEIR CHILDREN HAD?

The usual answer to this riddle is, of course, 'two parents'. But another possible answer is 'navels'. Although paintings of Adam and Eve show them with navels, the question has often been asked: why would Adam and Eve have navels if they were created rather than born? As God's creations, they would not have had umbilical cords.

ADAM AND EVE WERE VEGETARIANS

In Genesis 1:29, God says to Adam and Eve:
Behold, I have given you every herb bearing seed and every tree, in
which is the fruit yielding seed; to you it shall be for meat.
It was not until after the Flood that people were permitted by God to
kill animals for food:
Every moving thing that liveth shall be meat for you; even as the green
herb have I given you all things (Genesis 9:3).

Adam lived to the age of 930 (Genesis 5:5). The Bible does not tell us how old Eve was when she died. Although there is no biblical record of where they died, there is a legend that Adam was buried at the place that would later become Calvary, so that he would be the first to be redeemed by the blood of Christ.

CREATIONISM

❖Creationism is the belief that the universe and everything in it has its origin in specific deliberate acts of creation by God, as recorded in the Book of Genesis. Creationists do not believe that life developed by natural processes such as are postulated in Charles Darwin's theory of evolution, and most do not accept the Big Bang theory of the origin of the universe. Creationism takes several different forms:

❖The basic premise of Intelligent Design is that the world we live in and all the life-forms it contains show overwhelming evidence of having been designed by some higher being (i.e. God), and could not possibly have come about merely by chance or random evolution.

❖Creation science can be seen as the scientific wing of creationism. It tries to prove that the account of creation in Genesis is accurate and in complete accord with true science. One of the main focuses of its attack is on perceived weaknesses in the theory of evolution.

❖According to Young Earth Creationism, the universe and all that is in it was created somewhere between 6,000 and 10,000 years ago, in six 24-hour days, exactly in accordance with the Book of Genesis.

❖According to Old Earth Creationism, on the other

hand, the universe may well be billions of years old. It is possible to hold this belief and also a firm belief in the truth of the Bible. There are a number of different positions held within Old Earth Creationism. For example:

In the Day-Age version, it is argued that the 'days' of Genesis 1 are in fact long periods of time, not periods of 24 hours. Supporters of Day-Age Creationism may quote the Second Letter of Peter in support of their position: 'One day is with the Lord as a thousand years' (2 Peter 3:8). This, they believe, justifies their view that a 'day' in a biblical context need not mean a period of 24 hours. This view is also known as Progressive Creationism.

According to the Gap theory of Old Earth Creationism, the Genesis events did occur during actual 24-hour days, but there was a long gap between the creation of the earth (Genesis 1:1) and the rest of creation (Genesis 1:2 onwards).

Creationist museums

There are a number of museums, especially in North America, dedicated to explaining and promoting the creationist position, especially young earth creationism. In some exhibits, human beings and dinosaurs can be seen together.

THE SCOPES TRIAL

In Dayton, Tennessee, in 1925, a school teacher, John Scopes, was put on trial for violating state law by teaching the theory of evolution. He was convicted and fined $100.

Recent surveys have shown that over 50% of Americans believe in creation rather than evolution.

THE GARDEN OF EDEN

And the Lord God planted a garden eastward in Eden (Genesis 2:8).

◆ Eden is not the garden itself, the garden is *in* Eden. Many Bible scholars believe that the word 'Eden' is related to the Sumerian word *edin*, meaning 'a plain'.

◆ The garden was watered by a river, which split into four outside Eden. The four rivers it became are named, in the King James Version of the Bible, the Pison, the Gihon, the Hiddekel and the Euphrates. Bible scholars are not in agreement about the identification of the Pison and the Gihon, but the Hiddekel has been identified as the River Tigris, so the Hiddekel and the Euphrates form the boundaries of Mesopotamia. For this reason, some scholars have suggested that Eden was situated in southern Mesopotamia (i.e. modern Iraq). Others have suggested a site further north, around where the Tigris and Euphrates have their sources.

◆ 'Cush' which is translated 'Ethiopia' (Genesis 2:13) probably denotes an area close to the Black Sea, not Ethiopia in Africa.

◆ Eden is also called the 'garden of God' (Ezekiel 28:13 and 31:9) and the 'garden of the LORD' (Isaiah 51:3).

Paradise

In the Greek translation of the Old Testament known as the Septuagint (see page 15), the Hebrew word for 'garden' in Genesis 2:8 and 'Eden' in Isaiah 51:3 is translated into Greek as 'paradeisos', a word that comes from Old Persian *pairidaeza*, meaning 'park' or 'pleasure ground'.

EDEN IN AMERICA?

The Church of Jesus Christ of Latter-Day Saints believes that the Garden of Eden was in the western part of the state of Missouri in the United States. This, they believe, was revealed to the prophet Joseph Smith.

THE FALL

Of Man's first disobedience, and the fruit
Of that forbidden tree whose mortal taste
Brought death into the World, and all our woe ...

The infernal serpent; he it was, whose guile,
Stirr'd up with envy and revenge, deceived
The mother of mankind.
(John Milton, *Paradise Lost*)

✳

And when the woman saw that the tree was good for food, and that it was
pleasant to the eyes, and a tree to be desired to make one wise, she took of the
fruit thereof, and did eat, and gave also unto her husband with her; and he did eat.
(Genesis 3:1)

WHY AN APPLE?

Nowhere in the Bible is it said that the fruit that Adam and Eve ate was an apple. Although we cannot be sure who was the first to refer to the fruit of the forbidden tree as an apple, there are certainly many examples in English, dating back more than 1000 years. Here are two:

Adam brake goddis commandement of the appil.
(*Cursor Mundi*, from the year 1300)

✳

Him by fraud I have seduced
From his Creator ... with an apple.
(John Milton, *Paradise Lost*)

Adam's apple

The projection formed by the larynx at the front of the throat is called the Adam's apple because of a legend that when Adam ate the forbidden fruit, a piece of it stuck in his throat.

ADAM AND EVE AND ANAESTHESIA

It is sometimes said that when Sir James Simpson first used chloroform in the 19th century to relieve the pains of childbirth, ministers objected on the grounds that God had told Eve that 'in sorrow thou shalt bring forth children' (Genesis 3:16). Simpson is said to have countered this argument by pointing out that God also used anaesthesia when, in creating Eve, He 'caused a deep sleep to fall upon Adam' before removing his rib (Genesis 2:21).

This story is sometimes quoted by non-Christians as an example of the Church's hostility to scientific progress, but historical investigation has shown that anaesthesia was in fact warmly welcomed by churchmen of all denominations.

THE FIRST CLOTHES

And they knew that they were naked; and they sewed fig leaves together, and made themselves aprons. (Genesis 3:7)

APRONS OR BREECHES?
The version of the Bible known as the Geneva Bible, published in Geneva in 1560, is sometimes known as the 'Breeches Bible'. Its translation of Genesis 3:7 reads 'they sowed figge-tree leaves together and made themselves breeches'.

SOMETHING BETTER THAN LEAVES
Adam and Eve were not forced to wear fig-leaves for very long. Before driving them out of the Garden of Eden, God made coats of skins for them (Genesis 3:21). John Wycliffe (see page 14) also wrote of 'breeches'.

ADAM'S NEEDLE
The name Adam's needle is given to some plants that have needle-like spines, especially to species of Yucca which have long, narrow, spine-tipped leaves.

THE PROTEVANGELIUM
In Genesis 3:15, God tells the serpent: 'I will put enmity between thee and the woman, and between thy seed and her seed; it shall bruise thy head, and thou shalt bruise his heel'. This is seen as the earliest announcement of the Gospel, and is known as the Protevangelium, the 'first gospel'.

THE FIRST FAMILY

Only three of Adam and Eve's children are mentioned by name in the Bible: their first three sons Cain, Abel and Seth. Seth was the ancestor of Noah, who built the Ark and survived the Flood.

Adam had other sons and some daughters (Genesis 5:4), but their names are not recorded in the Bible. In the non-biblical Jewish book known as Jubilees, written perhaps c. 100BC, it is said that Cain married one of his sisters, whose name was Awan, and that Seth married another sister, Azura. (Jubilees also states that Adam and Eve had nine more sons.)

THE FIRST MURDER

Abel is a shepherd, and Cain is a crop-farmer (Genesis 4:2). Cain and Abel both offer sacrifices to God – Cain some of his harvest, Abel the best of his lambs. For reasons that are not made clear in the Genesis story, God accepts Abel's sacrifice but rejects Cain's. (The writer of the letter to the Hebrews says, in 11:4, that 'by faith Abel offered unto God a more excellent sacrifice than Cain'.)

In any case, angered by this rejection, Cain kills Abel, and as punishment is made 'a fugitive and a vagabond', living in the land of Nod, somewhere to the east of Eden.

When God asks Cain where Abel is, Cain responds with the famous question 'Am I my brother's keeper?'

The land of Nod

'Nod' means 'wandering'. Its name suggests that it was a country where people lived a nomadic existence.

THE MARK OF CAIN

Having murdered his brother, Cain is sure that he himself will be murdered. But God assures him that 'whosoever slayeth Cain, vengeance shall be taken on him sevenfold. And the Lord set a mark upon Cain, lest any finding him should kill him' (Genesis 4:15).

AS OLD (AND AS LARGE) AS METHUSELAH

The ages of the patriarchs (Genesis 5)

And all the days that Adam lived were nine hundred and thirty years: and he died.
And all the days of Seth were nine hundred and twelve years.
And all the days of Enos were nine hundred and five years.
And all the days of Cainan were nine hundred and ten years.
And all the days of Mahalaleel were eight hundred ninety and five years.
And all the days of Jared were nine hundred sixty and two years.
And all the days of Enoch were three hundred sixty and five years.
And all the days of Methuselah were nine hundred sixty and nine years.
And all the days of Lamech were seven hundred seventy and seven years.
And all the days of Noah were nine hundred and fifty years.

(The capacities sometimes vary according to the type of wine.)

Large bottle sizes named after Biblical characters

Bottle name	Capacity equivalent to:	Named after ...
JEROBOAM	4 ordinary bottles	Jeroboam, king of Israel (1 Kings 11:31)
REHOBOAM	6 ordinary bottles	Rehoboam, son of Solomon, king of Judah (1 Kings 11:43)
METHUSELAH	8 ordinary bottles	Methuselah, patriarch (Genesis 5:27)
SALMANAZAR	12 ordinary bottles	Shalmaneser, king of Assyria (2 Kings 17:3)
BALTHAZAR	16 ordinary bottles	Belshazzar, king of Babylon (Daniel 5.1)
NEBUCHADNEZZAR	20 ordinary bottles	Nebuchadnezzar, king of Babylon (2 Kings 24:1)
MELCHIOR	24 ordinary bottles	Melchior, name given in legend to one of the Magi (Matthew 2:1)
SOLOMON	28 ordinary bottles	Solomon, king of Israel (1 Kings 2:12)
MELCHIZEDEK	40 ordinary bottles	Melchizedek, king of Salem (Genesis 14:18)

NOAH AND THE FLOOD

THE REASON FOR THE FLOOD

God saw that the wickedness of man was great in the earth. God looked upon the earth, and, behold, it was corrupt and filled with violence. (Genesis 6: 5, 12–13)

And the Lord said: I will destroy man whom I have created from the face of the earth; both man, and beast, and the creeping thing, and the fowls of the air; for it repenteth me that I have made them. (Genesis 6:7)

*But Noah found grace in the eyes of the Lord.
Noah was a just man and perfect in his generations,
And Noah walked with God.* (Genesis 6:8–9)

And God said to Noah: Make thee an ark. (Genesis 6:14)

WHAT IS AN ARK?

'Ark' is simply an old English word for a boat. In Exodus 2:3, for example, we read that Moses' mother made 'an ark of bulrushes' for her baby son.

A modern Ark

Planet Ark is an Australian environmental organization founded in 1991. It encourages organizations and individuals to reduce their impact on the environment and provides a 'World Environment News' service.

GOD'S SPECIFICATIONS FOR THE ARK:

✳ Made from gopherwood (probably = cypress wood), and waterproofed with tar
✳ Length – 300 cubits (approx. = 450 feet or 137 metres)
✳ Breadth – 50 cubits (approx. = 75 feet or 23 metres)
✳ Height – 30 cubits (approx. = 45 feet or 14 metres)
✳ 1 window – 1 cubit (approx. = 18 inches or 45 centimetres); but in fact this was not necessarily a single window, but an opening between the deck and the roof, all the way round the ark)
✳ 1 door
✳ 3 decks

WHO SAILED IN THE ARK?

Eight people: Noah, Noah's wife, their sons Shem, Ham and Japheth, and his sons' wives.

… AND WHAT DID THEY TAKE WITH THEM?

According to Genesis 6:19, they took two of every sort of living creature, male and female. However Chapter 7:2–3 specifies seven (or seven pairs) of birds and of ritually clean animals, but one pair of ritually unclean animals. God also tells Noah what food to take for his family and the animals : 'Take thou unto thee of all food that is eaten … and it shall be for food for thee, and for them'.

THE FLOOD

THE FLOOD COMES

In the six hundredth year of Noah's life, on the seventeenth day of the second month all the 'fountains of the great deep' and the 'windows of heaven' open. And it rains over the earth for forty days and forty nights. All the hills and mountains are covered. And all living creatures on the earth die. The water covers the earth for a hundred and fifty days.

THE RAIN STOPS AND THE WATERS START TO ABATE

God then causes a wind to blow over the earth, and the waters start to drop. The 'fountains of the deep' are closed and the rain stops falling. After a hundred and fifty days the water level begins to drop. And the ark comes to rest on the mountains of Ararat.

NOAH SENDS OUT BIRDS TO LOOK FOR DRY LAND

After forty days, Noah opens the window of the ark, and sends out a raven, which doesn't come back but flies to and fro until the water dries up. He also sends out a dove to see if the water has gone down, but the dove can't find anywhere to land because there is still water over the whole earth, and it returns to the ark.

Seven days later, Noah sends out the dove again. When the dove comes back to him in the evening, it is holding an olive leaf in its beak, so Noah knows that the water has gone down. He waits another seven days, and sends out the dove again; this time it doesn't come back.

THE LAND DRIES OUT

In the six hundredth and first year, on the first day of the first month, Noah removes the covering of the ark, and looks out, and, sure enough, the ground is dry. The flood is over.

Another Flood story

Another story of the Flood is found in the literature of several ancient Middle-Eastern cultures. In the 'Epic of Gilgamesh', King Gilgamesh meets Utnapishtim, the 'Noah' figure in the story. Utnapishtim tells Gilgamesh that the gods decided to unleash a flood to destroy the people on earth. However, Utnapishtim was warned by the god Ea to build a boat.

Utnapishtim did not do all the work himself; he had craftsmen working for him. The upper deck measured 120 cubits by 120 cubits (180 feet or 55 metres), and there were six lower decks. When it was launched, Utnapishtim took on board his family and kinsfolk, and the craftsmen, and tame and wild animals.

When the storm came, it lasted six days and nights, then subsided. When Utnapishtim looked out, there was utter silence: all mankind had turned to clay. When the boat came to rest, on Mount Nisir, Utnapishtim sent out a dove and a swallow, which both returned to the boat, and then a raven, which didn't come back. Then he opened up the boat.

FOUR OLD TESTAMENT COVENANTS

THE COVENANT WITH NOAH (Genesis 9)

After the Flood God tells Noah and his sons to 'be fruitful, and multiply, and replenish the earth'. He makes a covenant with Noah, his sons, their descendants, and all living creatures, promising never again to cause a flood that will destroy the earth. As a sign of this covenant, whenever rain clouds appear, God will put a rainbow in the sky and it will remind him of his promise.

THE COVENANT WITH ABRAHAM (Genesis 15 and 17)

God promises Abraham that his descendants will be as numerous as the stars in the sky, and that they will occupy the land of Canaan 'from the river of Egypt unto the great river, the river Euphrates'. Many years later, when Abraham is 99 years old, God again promises that he will be the 'father of many nations', that his descendants will have 'all the land of Canaan, for an everlasting possession', and that he will be their God. As a physical sign of this covenant, Abraham and all his male descendants must be circumcised.

THE COVENANT WITH MOSES AND THE ISRAELITES (Exodus 19–24)

When the Israelites set up camp at Sinai, God tells Moses to tell them that if they will obey him and keep his covenant, they will be his chosen people (19:5). When Moses reads out God's commandments to the Israelites, they agree to obey them: 'All that the Lord hath said will we do, and be obedient'. Moses then sprinkles blood on the people, saying, 'Behold the blood of the covenant, which the Lord hath made with you concerning all these words' (24:8).

THE COVENANT WITH DAVID (2 Samuel 7)

Through the prophet Nathan, God promises King David that his 'throne shall be established for ever', that is, that there will always be one of his descendants on the throne of Israel.

... AND THE PROMISE OF A NEW COVENANT TO COME

Some 400 years later, through the prophet Jeremiah, God promises Israel a new covenant (Jeremiah 31:31–34):

Behold, the days come, saith the Lord, that I will make a new covenant with the house of Israel, and with the house of Judah: Not according to the covenant that I made with their fathers in the day that I took them by the hand to bring them out of the land of Egypt; which my covenant they brake, although I was an husband unto them, saith the Lord: But this shall be the covenant that I will make with the house of Israel; After those days, saith the Lord, I will put my law in their inward parts, and write it in their hearts; and will be their God, and they shall be my people. And they shall teach no more every man his neighbour, and every man his brother, saying, Know the Lord: for they shall all know me, from the least of them unto the greatest of them, saith the Lord; for I will forgive their iniquity, and I will remember their sin no more.

This future covenant promised by God is seen by Christians (as for example in Hebrews 8:6–17) as being fulfilled in the new covenant established by Jesus by his death on the Cross.

WINE IS A MOCKER, STRONG DRINK IS RAGING
(Proverbs 20:1)

According to Genesis 9:21, Noah is the first person to get drunk. In his drunken stupor, he falls asleep naked, and his son Ham discovers him in this state. Ham tells his brothers, who pick up a robe, and carrying it between them, carefully walk backwards to Noah and, without looking at him, cover him up. When Noah sobers up, he is furious with Ham, and on this basis curses Canaan, Ham's son, saying that he will be the servant of Shem and Japheth (9:26–27). This is seen by many as a prophetic statement, foretelling the conquest of Canaan by the Israelites (descendants of Shem through his son Arphaxad – see page 92).

ALCOHOL IS FORBIDDEN TO AARON AND HIS SONS:

And the Lord spake unto Aaron, saying, Do not drink wine nor strong drink, thou, nor thy sons with thee, when ye go into the tabernacle of the congregation, lest ye die: it shall be a statute for ever throughout your generations. (Leviticus 10:8–9)

ALCOHOL IS NOT FOR KINGS:

It is not for kings to drink wine; nor for princes strong drink: Lest they drink, and forget the law, and pervert the judgment of any of the afflicted. (Proverbs 31:4)

BUT THE BIBLE WRITERS ARE NOT UNAWARE OF THE BENEFITS OF ALCOHOLIC DRINK, WISELY USED:

Give strong drink unto him that is ready to perish, and wine unto those that be of heavy hearts. Let him drink, and forget his poverty, and remember his misery no more. (Proverbs 31: 6–7)

Drink no longer water, but use a little wine for thy stomach's sake and thine often infirmities. (1 Timothy 5:23)

THE DISUNITED NATIONS

The Tower of Babel

Babel (from *Bab-Ili* = 'gate of God') was in the land of Shinar, which is Babylonia, and it is there that mankind, in order to make a name for themselves, decided to build a tower that would reach up to heaven. To prevent this, God caused a confusing profusion of new languages, so that people could no longer understand one another and work together on the tower.

THE LANGUAGE OF ADAM AND EVE

Behold, the people is one, and they have all one language. (Genesis 11:6)

Yes, but what language? There have been a number of interesting attempts to answer this question, generally involving experiments on children:

• King James IV of Scotland (1473–1513) took two young children and put them in the care of a woman who was unable to talk, further isolating them by putting them all on an island. He was keen to know what language the children would speak, never having themselves been spoken to. According to the 16th-century historian, Robert Lindsay, it was said that they 'spoke good Hebrew', but he admits this is only hearsay.

• Frederick II (1194–1250), the Holy Roman Emperor, had tried something similar, but the experiment was a failure. A 7th-century BC Egyptian pharaoh, Psamtik I, had been more successful, however. Two babies were brought up by a shepherd who was to look after them but never speak to them. The first word the children spoke was, apparently, 'bekos', which Psamtik ascertained to be the Phrygian word for 'bread'.

• A 17th-century Swedish writer, Andreas Kempe, suggested, not entirely seriously, that in the Garden of Eden God spoke Swedish and Adam spoke Danish – and the serpent spoke French!

WHO BEGAT WHO? (Genesis 10)

DESCENDANTS OF JAPHETH

Gomer   *from Gomer: Ashkenaz, Riphath, Togarmah*
Magog
Madai
Javan   *from Javan: Elishah, Tarshish, Kittim, Dodanim*
Tubal
Meshech
Tiras

DESCENDANTS OF HAM

Cush   *from Cush: Seba, Havilah, Sabtah, Raamah, Sabtecha,*   *from Raamah: Sheba, Dedan*
           Nimrod
Mizraim   *from Mizraim: Ludim, Anamim, Lehabim, Naphtuhim,*   *from Casluhim: Philistim*
           Pathrusim, Casluhim, Caphtorim
Phut
Canaan   *from Canaan: Sidon, Heth, Jebusites, Amorites, Girgasites,*
           Hivites, Arkites, Sinites, Arvadites, Zemarites, Hamathites

DESCENDANTS OF SHEM

Elam
Asshur
Arphaxad   *from Arphaxad: Salah*   *from Salah: Eber*   *from Eber: Peleg, Joktan (Joktan's*
                                               descendants were Almodad, Sheleph,
                                               Hazar-maveth, Jerah, Hadoram,
                                                 Uzal, Diklah, Obal, Abimael, Sheba,
                                                 Ophir, Havilah, Jobab.)
Lud
Aram   *from Aram: Uz, Hul, Gether, Mash*

There is a Sheba and a Havilah among the descendants of both Ham and Shem; Lud is a son of Shem, but the Ludim are descended from Ham.

> Some of these peoples have been identified with reasonable certainty by scholars. For example:
>
> **GOMER**   =   *Cimmerians, a people originally from north of the Caucasus and the Ukraine, but later in what is now central Turkey.*
>
> **ASHKENAZ**   =   *Scythians, a warlike people from central Asia, noted*

		for their horsemanship; drove the Cimmerians out of the Ukraine
MADAI	=	*Medes (see page 38)*
JAVAN	=	*the people of Ionia, the coastal region of what is now western Turkey*
TARSHISH	=	*(possibly) the people of Spain; Jonah tried to flee to Tarshish*
KITTIM	=	*the people of Cyprus*
CUSH	=	*Ethiopians*
SHEBA	=	*the people of Saba (now Yemen)*
MIZRAIM	=	*(possibly) Egyptians*
LUDIM	=	*(possibly) the people of Lydia, in what is now western Turkey*
CAPHTORIM	=	*Cretans*
PHILISTIM	=	*Philistines (see page 38)*
PHUT	=	*Libyans*
HETH	=	*Hittites (see page 37)*
ASSHUR	=	*Assyria*
ARAM	=	*Arameans (see page 37)*

NIMROD, the son of Cush, is described as 'a mighty hunter'. His kingdom included Babel (= Babylon), Erech (= Uruk), Accad and Calneh, in the land of Shinar (= Babylonia, in southern Mesopotamia, now Iraq).

'Calneh' may not actually be the name of a city, but may mean something like 'all of these'.

PEOPLES AND LANGUAGES

Although Elam is listed as a son of Shem, modern linguists do not consider the Elamite language to have been a Semitic language, related to Hebrew, Aramaic and Arabic. It has even been suggested that Elamite is related to the languages of southern India, though this has not met with general acceptance.

FROM NOAH TO ABRAHAM

The patriarchs from Shem to Abraham's father Terah were also long-lived (Genesis 11), though not as long-lived as the earlier patriarchs from Adam to Noah:

Shem lived to the age of 600. His son Arphaxad lived till he was 438. His son Salah lived to the age of 433. Carrying on down the generations, Eber died at the age of 464, Peleg was 239 when he died, Reu lived to the age of 239, Serug to the age of 230, Nahor to the age of 148, and Terah to the age of 205.

NAMES FOR THE UNNAMED WIVES

The Bible does not tell us the names of the patriarchs' wives. Later non-Biblical tradition such as the book of Jubilees has, however, provided many of them with names (and their relationship to their husbands):

CAIN'S WIFE: Awan - *Cain and Seth's sister* ● SETH'S WIFE: Azura - *Cain and Seth's sister* ● ENOS'S WIFE: Noam - *Enos's sister* ● CAINAN'S WIFE: Mualeleth - *Cainan's sister* ● MAHALALEEL'S WIFE: Dinah - *daughter of his cousin Barakiel* ● JARED'S WIFE: Baraka - *daughter of his cousin Rasujal* ● ENOCH'S WIFE: Edna - *daughter of his cousin Danel* ● METHUSELAH'S WIFE: Edna - *daughter of his cousin Azrial* ● LAMECH'S WIFE: Betenos - *daughter of his cousin Baraki'il* ● NOAH'S WIFE: Emzara - *daughter of his cousin Rake'el* ● HAM'S WIFE: Ne'elatama'uk ● SHEM'S WIFE: Sedeqetelebab ● JAPHETH'S WIFE: Adataneses ● ARPHAXAD'S WIFE: Rasu'eja - *daughter of Susan, daughter of Elam*

There is an extra generation here, not mentioned in the Hebrew Bible, but found in the Greek Septuagint version (see also Luke 3:36): CAINAN'S WIFE: Melka - *daughter of Madai, son of Japheth*

● SALAH'S WIFE: Mu'ak - *his cousin* ● EBER'S WIFE: Azurad - *daughter of Nebrod* ● PELEG'S WIFE: Lomna - *daughter of Sina'ar* ● REU'S WIFE: Ora - *daughter of Ur, the son of Kesed* ● SERUG'S WIFE: Melka - *daughter of his cousin Kaber* ● NAHOR'S WIFE: Ijaska - *daughter of Nestag, a Chaldean* ● TERAH'S WIFE: Edna - *daughter of his cousin Abram*

ABRAHAM

FACTFILE	
Original name: ABRAM	UNNAMED CONCUBINES
Father: TERAH	*Children:* (BY SARAH) ISAAC; (BY HAGAR)
Mother: (ACCORDING TO THE BOOK OF JUBILEES)	ISHMAEL; (BY KETURAH) ZIMRAN, JOKSHAN,
EDNA	MEDAN, MIDIAN, ISHBAK AND SHUAH; (BY
Place of birth: UR, IN SOUTHERN	CONCUBINES) UNNAMED SONS
MESOPOTAMIA (NOW IRAQ)	*Brothers:* NAHOR AND HARAN
Wives, etc: SARAI (HIS HALF-SISTER; LATER	(HARAN DIED IN UR)
CALLED SARAH); KETURAH; HAGAR AND	*Nephew:* LOT (SON OF HARAN)

KEY EVENTS IN ABRAHAM'S LIFE

THE JOURNEY TO HARAN (GENESIS 11:31)
Terah leaves Ur with Abram, Sarai and
Lot to go to Canaan. Travelling north-
west, they reach the town of Haran, in
what is now south-eastern Turkey, and
stop there. Terah dies in Haran.

❖

THE JOURNEY TO CANAAN (12:1–5)
When Abram is seventy-five years old,
he leaves Haran with Sarai and Lot and
they travel south into Canaan. There God
appears to Abram and promises:

'I will make of thee a great nation'
(12:2) and 'Unto thy seed will I give
this land' (12:7).

❖

TO EGYPT AND BACK (12:10–13:12)
Because of a famine, Abram and his
family leave Canaan and journey south
to Egypt. There he and Sarai pretend
they are brother and sister rather than
husband and wife (not entirely a lie,
since Sarai was Abram's half-sister).
Innocently, Pharaoh takes Sarai into
his harem, for which he
is punished by God.
Abram, Sarai and Lot
return to Canaan, where
he and Lot part company.
Abram remains in
Canaan, while Lot moves
eastward to the Jordan
valley, near Sodom.

GOD REPEATS HIS PROMISE (15:18)

'Unto thy seed have I given this land, from the river of Egypt unto the great river, the river Euphrates.'

Abram was willing to put his trust in God (15:6).

HAGAR AND ISHMAEL (16)

Sarai has been unable to produce children, so she suggests that Abram take her maid Hagar as a wife. Hagar bears a son, and Abram names him Ishmael. Abram is now eighty-six years old.

❖

FROM ABRAM TO ABRAHAM (17:1–11)

When Abram is ninety-nine years old, the Lord appears to him and says:

'Thou shalt be a father of many nations. Neither shall thy name any more be called Abram, but Abraham. As for Sarai thy wife, Sarah shall her name be.'

Abram means 'exalted father'; Abraham means 'father of a multitude'. Sarah means 'princess'.

As a sign of the covenant between God and Abraham, all men and boys are from now on to be circumcised (Genesis 17:9–14).

❖

ISAAC (17–18, 21–22)

God promises Abraham that he and Sarah will have a son, at which Abraham laughs, thinking it impossible that a 100-year-old man and a 90-year-old woman could have a child. But they do have a son, named Isaac. When Isaac is a boy, God tests Abraham's faith, telling him to take his son to Moriah and there offer him up in sacrifice. Abraham does as he is commanded, and is just about to kill his son when the Lord stops him. When Abraham looks round, he sees a ram caught in some bushes. This Abraham offers up as a burnt offering instead of Isaac.

Many people believe that the hill where the sacrifice took place is one of the hills of Jerusalem, perhaps even the Temple hill.

❖

DEATHS OF SARAH AND ABRAHAM (23, 25)

Sarah and Abraham are buried near Hebron.

ABRAHAM'S BOSOM

A name for heaven, used in the parable of the rich man and the beggar (Luke 16:22) and by Shakespeare:

'The sons of Edward sleep in Abraham's bosom' (Richard III 4:iii).

CIRCUMCISION

The origin of the practice of circumcision is given in Genesis 17:9–14, where it is a sign of the covenant between God and Abraham. God lays down that every male is to be circumcised, and not only Israelites but also their non-Israelite servants. Every male child is to be circumcised when he is eight days old.

> ### Shechem
> When Shechem the Hivite prince asks to be allowed to marry Jacob's daughter Dinah (Genesis 34), her brothers will only agree to it if he and all the males in his city are circumcised. This Shechem persuades his fellow Hivites to do. Dinah's brothers, however, are actually only out for revenge, as Shechem has already raped their sister. While Shechem and his men 'were still sore', the sons of Jacob kill them all and plunder the city.

✿ That circumcision was not merely an outward sign of the covenant but also an indication of an inward commitment is shown by Deuteronomy 10:

And now, Israel, what doth the Lord thy God require of thee, but to fear the Lord thy God, to walk in all his ways, and to love him, and to serve the Lord thy God with all thy heart and with all thy soul, to keep the commandments of the Lord, and his statutes? Circumcise therefore the foreskin of your heart, and be no more stiffnecked.

Similarly, the prophet Jeremiah (6:10) speaks of those who will not listen to God as having 'uncircumcised ears'.

✿ Circumcision continues until the time of the Exodus, as God instructs Moses and Aaron (Exodus 12:43–49) that only males who have been circumcised may eat the Passover meal. However, the practice lapses during the Israelites' 40 years in the wilderness: according to Joshua 5:5, all the men who had come out of Egypt had been circumcised, but those born in the wilderness had not been. God therefore instructs Joshua that all male Israelites should be now circumcised.

✡ King Antiochus IV (175–164BC) tried to stamp out the Jewish religion. Among the things he banned was circumcision. It is recorded in 2 Maccabees 6, in the Apocrypha, that two women who circumcised their children were paraded round Jerusalem with their babies hanging at their breasts, and were then thrown from the city walls.

✡ The only other recorded example of a woman circumcising a child is in Exodus 4, where in an unexplained incident in which God tries to kill Moses as he returns with his family to Egypt, Zipporah, Moses' wife, circumcises their son and touches Moses' feet with the foreskin. Why Moses had not already circumcised his son is also not explained.

CIRCUMCISION AND THE CHURCH

The early church was for a time divided over whether or not non-Jewish converts to Christianity should be required to be circumcised. Some Judaean Christians in Antioch argued that non-Jews had to be circumcised in order to be saved (Acts 15:1). The matter was referred back to the church in Jerusalem, where some former Pharisees also argued that Gentile converts had to be circumcised and had to obey the Mosaic Law. The 'apostles and elders' met to discuss the problem, and Peter spoke out strongly against it, as no doubt did Paul.
The decision of the church leaders was that there was no need for Gentile Christians to be circumcised or to obey the Law.

'Circumcision' and 'uncircumcision' sometimes denote 'Jews' and 'Gentiles': Paul writes to the Galatians (2:7) that he was to preach the gospel to the 'uncircumcision' just as Peter was to go to the 'circumcision'.

WHO WERE THE PHARAOHS OF THE BIBLE?

Egyptian pharaohs are mentioned several times in the Bible, sometimes playing a major role in the history of the Israelites and sometimes only mentioned in passing. It is not always possible to say with certainty which pharaoh is meant in a particular passage of the Bible, but the following suggestions have been made for those of most importance in Bible history:

The pharaoh who took Sarah into his harem, not knowing she was Abraham's wife (Genesis 12), would have been one of the pharaohs by the name of Amenemhat or Sesostris who ruled Egypt about 1900BC.

❖

The pharaoh who promoted Joseph was probably one of the Hyksos, Semitic rulers of Egypt between c. 1674 and 1567BC.

❖

The exodus of the Israelites from Egypt probably took place c. 1300BC, and it is thought that the pharaoh may have been Ramses II, who ruled from 1304 to 1237BC.

❖

Who the pharaoh was who 'knew not Joseph' and whose daughter adopted Moses

is not clear, but if the exodus took place c. 1300BC and Moses was 80 years old at the time (Exodus 7:7), one can calculate back to one of the pharaohs who ruled Egypt shortly before the famous Tutankhamun, who ruled from 1360 to 1350BC.

❖

The pharaoh who captured the town of Gezer and gave it to 'his daughter, King Solomon's wife' (1 Kings 9:16) was probably Siamun, who ruled from 978 to 959BC.

❖

The Shishak, king of Egypt, to whom Jeroboam fled (1 Kings 11:40) and who 'came up against Jerusalem' and Rehoboam (1 Kings 14:25) was Sheshonq I, pharaoh from 945 to 924BC.

SODOM AND GOMORRAH

When Abraham and Lot part company, Lot moves his family and flocks east, settling somewhere near the city of Sodom – perhaps unwisely, because *'the men of Sodom were wicked and sinners before the Lord exceedingly'* (Genesis 13:13).

❖

Sodom and Gomorrah were two of the 'cities of the plain', five cities – Sodom, Gomorrah, Admah, Zeboiim and Zoar – in the valley of Siddim (Genesis 14:2–3).

Their exact position has never been established, but they were close to the Dead Sea (14:3). Indeed, it has been suggested the cities may actually now be under the southern end of the Dead Sea. The valley of Siddim was full of tar pits (KJV 'slimepits').

❖

God tells Abraham that he intends to destroy Sodom for its wickedness, but at Abraham's pleading, agrees not to do so if even ten righteous men can be found in the city. A rather unsavoury incident follows in which the men of Sodom demand to have sex with two men who are Lot's guests, and who are in fact angels. This establishes by implication that there aren't even ten righteous men there. The angels warn Lot to get his family out of Sodom before God destroys the city, and they flee to nearby Zoar.
'Then the Lord rained upon Sodom and upon Gomorrah brimstone and fire'
(Genesis 19:24).

❖

The angels had warned Lot that he and his family should not look back as they flee from Sodom. However, Lot's wife does look back, and she becomes a 'pillar of salt'.

Jesus alludes to this incident in Luke's gospel (17:29–30):
But the same day that Lot went out of Sodom it rained fire and brimstone from heaven, and destroyed them all. Even thus shall it be in the day when the Son of man is revealed.

FROM CANAAN TO EGYPT

Abraham's son Isaac had two sons, Esau and Jacob. They were twins, but Esau was the firstborn. However, he sold his birthright to Jacob for some lentil stew ('red pottage' in the KJV). We are told that Isaac preferred Esau, but his wife Rebekah preferred Jacob. When the time comes for Isaac, now old and blind, to pass on his blessing to Esau as the oldest son, Jacob and Rebekah trick him into blessing Jacob instead.

JACOB'S LADDER

Jacob then flees to Haran. On his way there, while asleep one night, he has a vision of a stairway (a 'ladder' in the KJV) reaching from earth to heaven, with angels going up and down it. Jacob sees God at the top of the stairway. Repeating the promise he has made to Abraham, God tells Jacob: 'the land whereon thou liest, to thee will I give it, and to thy seed' (Genesis 29:13). Jacob takes the stone he was using as a pillow and sets it up as a memorial pillar, and names the place Bethel, 'the House of God'.

THE STONE OF DESTINY

According to an ancient tradition, the stone that Jacob used as a pillow was taken to Egypt by his sons. From there it was supposedly carried to Spain, and from there to Ireland. It was the stone that Irish kings were crowned on, and was known as the 'fatal stone' or 'stone of destiny'. From Ireland, according to the legend, it was taken to Scotland, and was the stone on which Scottish kings were crowned down to the end of the 13th century. In 1296, King Edward I of England took the stone to Westminster Abbey in London, where it became part of the Coronation Chair. It was returned to Scotland in 1996.

JACOB BECOMES 'ISRAEL'

Many years later, Jacob, now married to his two cousins Leah and Rachel, and with a large family, returns from Haran to Canaan. While encamped at the river Jabbok, Jacob wrestles all night with a being who he eventually recognizes is God. God tells him that his name will no longer be Jacob, but Israel, which means 'God struggles' or 'he struggles with God' (Genesis 32:28).

Israel's twelve sons	
BY LEAH:	Reuben, Simeon, Levi, Judah, Issachar, Zebulun (and a daughter, Dinah)
BY RACHEL'S MAID BILHAH:	Dan, Naphtali
BY LEAH'S MAID ZILPAH:	Gad, Asher
BY RACHEL:	Joseph, Benjamin

Israel's sons became the patriarchs of tribes of Israel (Genesis 49:28). Later, however, while the tribe of Levi is spread throughout the whole nation, Joseph's sons Ephraim and Manasseh are tribal patriarchs (see e.g. Numbers 1), so maintaining the number 'twelve'.

JOSEPH AND THE COAT OF MANY COLOURS

Joseph, the second-youngest son, was his father's favourite, and his brothers hated him for it. Jacob even gives Joseph a particularly fine coat (a coat of many colours according to the KJV).

Sadly, Joseph may not have had a coat of many colours. The exact meaning of the Hebrew words is not clear. It may have been a coat with long, wide sleeves. However, it was clearly something special, perhaps a richly decorated coat, an indication of Jacob's particular love of Joseph.

JOSEPH AND THE AMAZING TECHNICOLOR DREAMCOAT, *the Andrew Lloyd Webber and Tim Rice production of the story of Joseph, was first performed as a 15-minute school production in 1968.*

Joseph sold as a slave

Not only is Joseph his father's favourite, he has dreams in which it seems that he is going to be lord over the rest of his family. He sees a harvest scene in which the sheaves of corn his brothers cut bow down before the sheaf that he has cut, and he sees the sun, moon and eleven stars bowing to him. His brothers have had enough, and plot to kill him. However, they come up with a better plan and sell him to some traders who take Joseph to Egypt and sell him as a slave. Through his God-given ability to interpret dreams Joseph comes to the attention of the pharaoh, whom he warns about an impending seven-year famine. As a result, the pharaoh makes Joseph his senior court official.

JACOB AND HIS FAMILY COME TO EGYPT (GENESIS 42–46)

When the famine comes, Egypt is prepared for it. Grain has been stockpiled during the preceding years. But famine also hits Canaan. Hearing that there is grain available in Egypt, Joseph's brothers travel down to buy supplies. Joseph recognizes them, but they do not recognize him until he reveals himself to them. Joseph has forgiven his brothers, realizing that, even though they did not know it at the time, all that has happened was part of God's plan to save Jacob and his family.

The pharaoh tells Joseph to send his brothers back to Canaan, to tell Jacob to bring his whole family down to Egypt, where they will be given the best land and will 'eat the fat of the land'. When Jacob and his family arrive in Egypt, they settle in Goshen, near the Nile delta.

THE DEATHS OF JACOB AND JOSEPH

When Jacob dies, his body is taken back to Canaan and buried at Machpelah, beside Abraham, Sarah, Isaac and Rebekah. When Joseph is dying, he asks that his bones be taken to Canaan when God leads the Israelites back to the land he has promised them.

MOSES AND THE TEN PLAGUES

The children of Israel were fruitful, and increased abundantly, and multiplied, and waxed exceeding mighty; and the land was filled with them (Exodus 1:7).

Some three hundred and fifty years have passed since the time of Joseph, and the Israelites are now seen as a threat:

> *There arose up a new king over Egypt, which knew not Joseph. And he said unto his people, Behold, the people of the children of Israel are more and mightier than we: Come on, let us deal wisely with them; lest they multiply, and it come to pass, that, when there falleth out any war, they join also unto our enemies, and fight against us* (Exodus 1:8–10).

The Israelites are enslaved, and the pharaoh rules that all Israelite boy babies must be killed.

MOSES, THE PRINCE OF EGYPT

Not wanting her son to be killed, Moses' mother hides him in a basket among some reeds on the river Nile. There he is found by the pharaoh's daughter, who takes him and brings him up as her son. She names the baby 'Moses' because she 'lifted him out of the water'.

Since it is not clear why an Egyptian princess would give her adopted baby a name that is based on a Hebrew pun (relating 'Moses' to a Hebrew word meaning 'lifted out'), it has been suggested that it may actually have been Moses' mother who gave him his name. On the other hand, some scholars have linked the name 'Moses' to Egyptian *ms* 'child'.

Some years later, as a young man, Moses comes upon an Egyptian and an Israelite fighting. He kills the Egyptian, but realizing he has been found out, flees to Midian, on the east of the Red Sea in what is now Saudi Arabia. There he marries Zipporah, the daughter of Jethro, the priest of Midian, and looks after his flocks.

THE BURNING BUSH

One day, when Moses has taken the flocks as far as Mount Horeb (which is Mount Sinai), he sees a bush, burning but not burning up. God speaks to him out of the bush, declaring himself to be the God of Abraham, Isaac and Jacob, whose name is I AM THAT I AM. God tells Moses that he is to go back to Egypt and lead the Israelites to Canaan, the 'land flowing with milk and honey'. When Moses protests that he is not an eloquent speaker and won't know what to say, God agrees to let his brother Aaron be his spokesman.

THE TEN PLAGUES

As expected, the pharaoh refuses to let the Israelites leave. And the plagues begin.

THE FIRST PLAGUE (EXODUS 7:14–25):
WATER TURNS INTO BLOOD
Following God's instructions, Aaron strikes the water of the river Nile, and the water turns to blood. The fish in the river die; and the river stinks, and the Egyptians cannot drink the water from the river.

Some scholars have considered whether God might have used natural phenomena to fulfil his purposes when afflicting Egypt with these terrible plagues. For example, the water turning to blood might have been caused by an abnormally high flood bringing large quantities of red earth down the River Nile, perhaps also with decaying algae and bacteria. If this is the case, this plague would have occurred about July or August, when the Nile floods.

✳

THE SECOND PLAGUE (8:1–15): FROGS
*Aaron stretches out his hand over the
waters of Egypt; and frogs appear
and cover the whole land of Egypt.
Then the frogs die. The Egyptians
gather them together into heaps, and
the whole country stinks.
Seven days later, there is a plague of frogs,
perhaps driven out of the polluted waters.*

❋

THE THIRD PLAGUE (8:16–19): LICE
*Next, God instructs Aaron to stretch
out his staff and strike the ground,
causing lice to appear.*

Modern translations of the Bible usually
speak of 'gnats' rather than 'lice'. The
gnats, or perhaps mosquitoes, might have
bred in the pools of stagnant water left by
the subsiding river.

In *Animals of Bible Lands*, the zoologist
George Cansdale suggests ticks as another
possibility.

❋

THE FOURTH PLAGUE (8:20–32): FLIES
*Next comes a huge swarm of flies.
The whole of Egypt is plagued with
flies, except Goshen where the
Israelites are living.*

❋

THE FIFTH PLAGUE (9:1–7): LIVESTOCK
DISEASE (MURRAIN IN THE KJV)
*The next plague is a disease that
causes the Egyptians' livestock to die
– their horses, asses, camels, oxen
and sheep. But the Israelites' livestock
is not affected: not one animal dies.*

Both anthrax and foot-and-mouth
disease have been suggested.

❋

THE SIXTH PLAGUE (9:8–12):
BOILS AND SORES
*God says to Moses to take handfuls of
ashes from a furnace, and toss them
into the air. The ashes spread like dust
over the whole of Egypt, causing an
outbreak of boils and sores that affect
both people and animals.*

Some scholars see a connection between
the plague of flies and the skin disease that
breaks out as boils and sores.

❋

THE SEVENTH PLAGUE (9:13–35): HAIL
*The next plague God sends is thunder
and hail and lightening. The hail is
so heavy, it flattens crops, destroys
trees and strikes down any person or
animal that is outside. Again, the
only place not affected is Goshen.*

Since the hail destroyed the flax and
barley, but not the wheat and 'rie' (or
spelt) (9: 31–2), this probably happened in
early February.

❋

THE EIGHTH PLAGUE (10:1–20): LOCUSTS
*The Lord causes an east wind to
blow, bringing with it a cloud of
locusts. There are so many locusts,
they cover the whole country, and
they eat everything: all the plants
and also any fruit which has
survived the hailstorm.*

THE NINTH PLAGUE (10:21–29): DARKNESS

Moses stretches out his hand towards heaven; and a thick darkness covers the whole country for three days.

Some scholars suggest this could have been a severe dust storm.

✳

THE TENTH PLAGUE (11, 12): DEATH OF THE FIRSTBORN SONS

The final plague settles the issue. At midnight the Lord kills all the firstborn sons throughout Egypt, from the firstborn of the pharaoh to the firstborn of the prisoner in his cells; even the firstborn of the Egyptians' livestock die. In the whole of Egypt there is not a house where someone has not died.

Some scholars have suggested a connection between the Egyptian plagues and the results of the eruption of the volcano on the Greek island of Thera or Santorini. However, since dates are uncertain, it is not clear whether such a connection can be justified: the two events may have been centuries apart.

The seven last plagues

In Revelation 15–16 'seven angels having the seven last plagues' are described. The angels pour over the earth the contents of seven bowls of God's anger, causing seven plagues not dissimilar to those inflicted on Egypt: horrible, painful sores ✳ the sea turning to blood, and everything in it dying ✳ rivers turning to blood ✳ the sun becoming scorchingly hot ✳ darkness ✳ the river Euphrates drying up ✳ thunder, lightning, an earthquake and hailstones.

THE JOURNEY TO CANAAN

The death of the Egyptian firstborn is the last straw: the Israelites are not only allowed to leave, they are told to leave! The exodus begins. The Israelites move out of Goshen, guided by a pillar of cloud during the day and a pillar of fire at night. There are 600,000 Israelite men, plus women, children and some others (a 'mixed multitude') who go with them.

As with the plagues, a connection has been suggested between the pillars of cloud and fire and the column of hot ash that would have been seen above the volcano at Thera, though this does not perhaps fit in with the movement of the pillar described in Exodus 14:19–20.

God has decided not to take the Israelites directly to Canaan through Philistine territory, although that would have been the shortest route, but rather by a more roundabout route through the desert. Which route the Israelites took is still a matter of debate.

PHARAOH'S ARMY GOT DROWNDED …

Moses stood on the Red Sea shore,
Smote the water with a two-by-four.
Pharaoh's army got drownded,
O Mary, don't you weep.
[Negro spiritual]

The Israelites have hardly departed before the Egyptians change their mind, and set off to bring back their slaves. Caught between the Red Sea and the Egyptian army, the Israelites panic. All except Moses. Following God's instructions, Moses holds his staff out over the sea, a strong wind blows up, and the waters part. The Israelites cross safely to the other side between walls of water, but when the Egyptians follow, the sea collapses over them.

Where was the 'Red Sea'?

Opinions differ. 'Red Sea' should certainly be 'Reed Sea', but where this sea of reeds was cannot be identified with certainty, nor can places mentioned in the story such as Migdol or Baal-zephon. One theory places the Reed Sea at the edge of the Mediterranean Sea, while another places it further south.

THE JOURNEY TO SINAI

From the Reed Sea, the Israelites journey to the Desert of Shur, which is situated to the north of the Sinai Peninsula. Over the following days, despite having already witnessed many miracles, the Israelites repeatedly show a surprising lack of faith in God, worrying and complaining about the lack of food and water. God, however, shows both his power and his care for his people: when they come to a bitter spring, he shows Moses how to make the water drinkable (Exodus 15:23); when there is no water to be had, God tells Moses to strike a rock with his stick, and when he does so, water gushes out (17:6); when there is no food to be had, God provides manna and quail to eat (16).

MANNA AND QUAIL

Manna (from Hebrew *man hu* 'what is it?') is described as being like a white coriander seed and tasting like wafers made with honey (Exodus 16:31). It appeared in the morning as the dew evaporated (16:13), and melted in the sunshine (16:21). It could be baked or boiled (16:23), but it went bad if too much was collected (16:20). No manna appeared on the Sabbath, however, and on the sixth day the Israelites could collect enough for two days. What exactly manna was is uncertain, though some scholars have suggested that it may have been something like the sweet substance called honeydew that is produced by scale insects on tamarisk bushes in Sinai.

Quail migrate each year between Africa and Eurasia, and would have crossed over the route taken by the Israelites. The quail arrived in the evening (16:13), perhaps suggesting that they were landing to rest during their migration, and the zoologist George Cansdale, in *Animals of Bible Lands*, notes that this still happens today.

THE TEN COMMANDMENTS

The next major event in the history of Israel takes place at Mount Sinai (the exact location of which is not certain). It is there that Moses receives from God the Ten Commandments (Exodus 20).

These are the Ten Commandments as given in Exodus 20:1–17:

And God spake all these words, saying,
I am the Lord thy God, which have brought thee out of the land of Egypt, out of the house of bondage.

1 Thou shalt have no other gods before me.

2 Thou shalt not make unto thee any graven image, or any likeness of any thing that is in heaven above, or that is in the earth beneath, or that is in the water under the earth: Thou shalt not bow down thyself to them, nor serve them: for I the Lord thy God am a jealous God, visiting the iniquity of the fathers upon the children unto the third and fourth generation of them that hate me; And shewing mercy unto thousands of them that love me, and keep my commandments.

3 Thou shalt not take the name of the Lord thy God in vain; for the Lord will not hold him guiltless that taketh his name in vain.

4 Remember the sabbath day, to keep it holy. Six days shalt thou labour, and do all thy work: But the seventh day is the sabbath of the Lord thy God: in it thou shalt not do any work, thou, nor thy son, nor thy daughter, thy manservant, nor thy maidservant, nor thy cattle, nor thy stranger that is within thy gates: For in six days the Lord made heaven and earth, the sea, and all that in them is, and rested the seventh day: wherefore the Lord blessed the sabbath day, and hallowed it.

5 Honour thy father and thy mother: that thy days may be long upon the land which the Lord thy God giveth thee.

6 Thou shalt not kill.

7 Thou shalt not commit adultery.

8 Thou shalt not steal.

9 Thou shalt not bear false witness against thy neighbour.

10 Thou shalt not covet thy neighbour's house, thou shalt not covet thy neighbour's wife, nor his manservant, nor his maidservant, nor his ox, nor his ass, nor any thing that is thy neighbour's.

✱ The Ten Commandments are also known as the Decalogue, from Greek *hoi deka logoi* 'the ten sayings'.

✱ The Ten Commandments are repeated in Deuteronomy 5:1–21. Although the wording of some verses is slightly different, the laws are the same. However, there are differences: while in the Exodus version, the fourth commandment is related to God having rested on the seventh day after creating the world, in the Deuteronomy version God specifies that no work is to be done on the Sabbath in order 'that thy manservant and thy maidservant may rest as well as thou' and that the Israelites are not to forget that they too were servants in Egypt (5:14–15). The

commandment is the same; only the focus is different.

✱ The numbering of the Commandments varies in different versions of the Bible (although the numbering always amounts to ten). The numbering in the table above reflects Protestant practice, whereas, following St Augustine, Roman Catholics and Lutherans have treated the injunction against worshipping other gods and making graven images as a single commandment and split the commandment against coveting into two.

✱ King Alfred the Great (849–901) introduced his Code of Saxon Laws with a shortened version of the Ten Commandments.

✱ Judaism recognizes a total of 613 commandments or *mitzvoth* in the Five Books of Moses: 248 positive ones which prescribe something (such as believing in God or walking in the ways of God) and 365 negative ones which proscribe something (such as worshipping other gods or allowing a sorcerer to live).

The Tablets of Stone and the Golden Calf

Moses spends 40 days and nights on Mount Sinai. Disheartened by this, the Israelites make a gold idol of a calf to have as their god (Exodus 32). When Moses comes down the mountain carrying the two stone tablets on which God has written the Ten Commandments, he finds the Israelites dancing round the idol. Furious, he throws down the stone tablets and breaks them. Then he grinds down the idol into powder, mixes it with water and makes the Israelites drink it.

According to Brewer's *Dictionary of Phrase and Fable*, there is a tradition that the golden calf is buried in Rook's Hill, near Chichester, in the south of England. However, the Bible is quite clear that Moses ground the calf into powder.

TWELVE THINGS THAT ARE FORBIDDEN IN THE MOSAIC LAW

eating meat with blood in it ◆ consulting mediums ◆ accepting bribes ◆ making false accusations ◆ using inaccurate weights and measures ◆ taking advantage of foreigners ◆ cursing someone who is deaf ◆ making a blind person stumble and fall ◆ sowing two different kinds of seed in one field ◆ making clothing with a mixture of wool and linen ◆ trimming beards ◆ tattoos murder ♦ kidnapping ♦ witchcraft ♦ blasphemy ♦ human sacrifice ♦ disobeying parents ♦ cursing parents ♦ hitting parents ♦ adultery ♦ incest ♦ homosexual sex ♦ sexual relations with animals

THE ARK OF THE COVENANT

Moses cuts two new tablets of stone and God writes out the Ten Commandments again (Exodus 34). The tablets are to be kept in a special box known as the ark of the Covenant (also called the ark of God, the ark of the Lord, the ark of the covenant of the Lord, and the ark of the testimony). The ark is made of acacia (shittim) wood, and is covered with gold inside and out (Exodus 25:10–11). It measures 2½ cubits long by 1½ cubits wide by 1½ cubits high (1 cubit = approximately 18 in or 45 cm). Its lid is of pure gold, and at each end of the lid is a gold cherub, the two cherubs facing one another and with their wings spread out over the box.

FORTY YEARS IN THE WILDERNESS

Twelve spies are sent into southern Canaan to assess the state of the country and the strength of its inhabitants. Forty days later the spies return, laden with grapes, pomegranates and figs, and report that the country is rich and fertile but, according to ten of the spies, the inhabitants are far too strong and the cities too well fortified to be attacked. (Two of the spies, Joshua and Caleb, disagree.) Disheartened yet again, the Israelites want to depose Moses and go back to Egypt. For this lack of faith, God condemns the Israelites to 40 more years in the wilderness.

The death of Moses

At the end of the Book of Deuteronomy, Moses is allowed by God to climb to the top of Mount Nebo and look into the Promised Land. Then, at the age of 120, Moses dies, and is buried in Moab. No one now knows where he is buried. Joshua is the new leader.

CANAAN: JOSHUA AND THE JUDGES

Now the Israelites are to cross the river Jordan into Canaan. In a miracle very similar to the one in which God parted the waters of the Reed Sea, the ark of the Covenant is carried into the river Jordan, the river stops flowing and the water piles up upstream at the town of Adam until all the Israelites have safely crossed over.

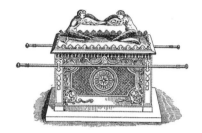

JOSHUA FOUGHT THE BATTLE OF JERICHO ...
... AND THE WALLS CAME A-TUMBLIN' DOWN

Jericho is the first Canaanite city to stand in the Israelites' way. Following God's commands, Joshua lines up the Israelites to march around the city walls. First come the men of war, followed by seven priests blowing ram's-horn trumpets, and then the ark of the Covenant. The rest of the Israelites bring up the rear. Once a day for six days, the Israelites march round the city, in complete silence apart from the sound of the trumpets. On the seventh day, they march round Jericho seven times. As commanded, the priests give a long blast on the trumpets, the people give a loud shout ... and the walls of Jericho collapse, as God had said they would. The Israelites kill the inhabitants and burn the city to the ground.

Joshua's curse

Joshua lays a curse on anyone who rebuilds the city: laying the foundations will cost his firstborn son, and setting up the gates will cost him his youngest son. Hiel of Bethel does rebuild the city (1 Kings 16), and it does cost the lives of his eldest son Abiram and his youngest son Segub.

Jericho as a city dates back to about 8000BC. It is said to be the oldest city in the world.

THE DIVISION OF THE LAND (Joshua 13–21)

East of the river Jordan, from the Dead Sea northwards: the tribes of Reuben, Gad and half of Manasseh (East Manasseh) ✳ *West of the Jordan, from the Dead Sea northwards:* the tribes of Simeon, Judah, Benjamin, Dan, Ephraim, half of Manasseh (West Manasseh), Issachar, Zebulun, Asher and Naphtali. (Dan later captured territory straddling the northernmost section of the Jordan.) ✳ *The tribe of Levi was assigned cities throughout the whole land.* ✳ *Ephraim and Manasseh were the sons of Joseph, not sons of Jacob/Israel.* ✳ *With the tribe of Levi not receiving any territory, there were twelve tribes with land either in Canaan or east of the Jordan.*

The Judges

The judges were national leaders and heroes who led the Israelites against enemies and oppressors after the death of Joshua.

Twelve judges are mentioned in the Book of Judges

Othniel ◆ Ehud ◆ Shamgar ◆ Deborah ◆ Gideon ◆ Tola ◆ Jair ◆ Jephthah ◆ Ibzan ◆ Elon ◆ Abdon ◆ Samson

The prophet Samuel and his sons are the last judges of Israel (1 Samuel 7–8).

GIDEON

With God's help, Gideon wins a great victory over the Midianites, Amalekites and desert tribesmen with only 300 men, whittled down according to God's instructions from an original 32,000 volunteers (Judges 7).

JEPHTHAH

Jephthah's victory over the Ammonites (Judges 11) turns to tragedy. Before the battle he vows to God that if he wins, he will sacrifice the first thing to come out of his house to meet him when he returns home. On his return, it is his only daughter who comes out to greet him. Jephthah is heartbroken, but his daughter insists he keep his vow, asking only that he wait two months so that she can grieve her death as a virgin.

SAMSON (Judges 13–16)

SAMSON AND THE PHILISTINES

At this time, Israel is under Philistine rule. Having killed a lion with his bare hands, Samson later sees that bees have nested in the carcass and there is honey in it. Thinking of this, Samson challenges some Philistines to answer this riddle:

From the eater came something to eat,
from the strong came something sweet.

Unable to answer the riddle, the men force Samson's wife to wheedle the answer out of him, which she does with her tears. When they now answer the riddle, Samson is obliged to give them new clothing – which he does by going out and killing some 30 other Philistines and taking their clothes. On another occasion, Samson kills 1,000 Philistines with the jawbone of a donkey; and on yet another occasion, he carries off the gates of the Philistine city of Gaza.

SAMSON AND DELILAH

Samson's undoing comes from a woman named Delilah. Before his birth, Samson was dedicated to God as a nazirite, and this is the source of his strength.

Nazirites did not drink wine or beer, did not shave or cut their hair, and were not allowed to touch dead bodies (Numbers 6).

Samson's immense strength remains with him only so long as his hair is not cut. This information Delilah eventually manages to coax out of him. Lulling Samson to sleep, she has his hair cut off, and Samson, now too weak to resist the Philistines, is blinded and carried off as a prisoner. But his hair grows again. Taken to the temple of the Philistine god Dagon, Samson prays to God for strength one last time, and his prayer granted, he brings down the temple, killing himself, the five Philistine kings and thousands of their people.

THE GIDEONS

Most people have come across a Gideons Bible somewhere. The Gideons International is an organization of Christian businessmen or professional men which distributes Bibles and New Testaments to such locations as hotels, schools, hospitals and prisons, and to members of the armed forces, the police, the fire service, etc.

The Gideons was set up in the United States in 1899 by three Christian commercial travellers – John H. Nicholson, Samuel E. Hill and Will J. Knights. They named themselves 'Gideons' after the Israelite leader Gideon in the Book of Judges (chapter 7) who with the help of God won a great battle with only a few men.

The Gideons became established in Canada in 1911, and in the British Isles in 1949.

GIDEON BIBLES

At a meeting of the organization in 1908, it was decided to undertake the placing of a Bible in every bedroom of every hotel throughout the United States, and this is the activity for which the Gideons are best known. In the hundred years that have passed since then, more than 1.3 billion Bibles and New Testaments have been distributed around the world.

The first 25 Bibles distributed by the Gideons were placed in the Superior Hotel, Iron Mountain, Montana, USA.

From Albania to Zimbabwe, from Afrikaans to Zulu

The Gideons International distributes Bibles in more than 80 languages in over 180 countries. On average, more than two copies of the Bible are now distributed every second.

In 1990, the Gideons presented their 500 millionth Bible to American president George Bush.

RUTH

There are only two books in the Old Testament and two books in the Apocrypha named after women: Ruth and Esther, and Judith and Susanna. The Apocrypha also includes additions to Esther.

Ruth and Orpah are Moabite girls, daughters-in-law of Naomi, a Jewish woman living in Moab. Naomi's husband has died, as have her two sons. Having first come to Moab with her husband and sons to escape a famine, Naomi hears that there is now corn in Judah, and she sets out to return to Bethlehem. Orpah remains in Moab, but Ruth insists on accompanying her mother-in-law.

Oprah Winfrey's name was meant to be Orpah.

The barley harvest is just beginning when Naomi and Ruth reach Bethlehem. Ruth goes out to gather barley that has been left in the fields by the reapers working for Boaz, a wealthy relative of Naomi's.

Leaving corn in the corners of fields, and any ears of corn that had been missed, for the poor to gather was a requirement of the Mosaic law (Leviticus 23:22).

Knowing who she is and what she has done for Naomi, Boaz takes special care of Ruth. She shares the workers' food, and Boaz even tells his reapers to deliberately pull barley out of the sheaves and leave it for Ruth to pick up. This continues throughout the summer. Then one day Naomi suggests to Ruth that she should find a husband. Ruth goes to Boaz and asks him to marry her. Boaz says he knows a closer relative who would be a more suitable husband, but agrees that if this man will not marry Ruth, he (Boaz) will. The man refuses, and Boaz marries Ruth. Ruth and Boaz have a son, Obed.

Obed was the father of Jesse, who was the father of King David.

SAUL, THE FIRST KING OF ISRAEL

King of Israel c.1050–1010BC
Tribe: BENJAMIN
Father: KISH
Wife: AHINOAM.
Concubine: RIZPAH
Sons: (BY AHINOAM) JONATHAN, ISHUI,
MELCHI-SHUA, ABINADAB, ESHBAAL; (BY
RIZPAH) ARMONI, MEPHIBOSHETH
Daughters: MERAB, MICHAL

KEY EPISODES IN THE LIFE OF SAUL

WHY A KING?

The prophet Samuel appointed his sons judges over Israel. However, angered by their corruption (1 Samuel 8:3), the Israelites ask Samuel for a king. With God's permission, Samuel agrees.

SAUL ANOINTED KING

The man chosen by God to be king is Saul, the tallest and most handsome man in Israel. While searching for some donkeys of his father's that have gone missing, Saul meets Samuel, and Samuel tells him he is the one God has chosen. Saul is anointed king.

SAUL'S DISOBEDIENCE

Samuel tells Saul to go to Gilgal and to wait there for seven days till he comes to offer sacrifice. However, faced with a Philistine army and with his own army deserting him, and with no sign of Samuel, Saul performs the sacrifice himself. When Samuel arrives, he tells Saul that for this disobedience to God, the kingship will pass out of his family (1 Samuel 13:13). Some time later, Samuel instructs Saul to attack the Amalekites and utterly destroy them and their property. However, Saul and his men keep the best of the plunder to offer to God. Samuel tells Saul that 'to obey is better than sacrifice' (1 Samuel 15:22), and that once again God has rejected him because of his disobedience.

THE DEATH OF SAUL

Defeated by the Philistines, Saul and his armour-bearer commit suicide (1 Samuel 31).

DAVID: SHEPHERD, GIANT-KILLER, PSALMIST, KING

<table>
<tr><td colspan="2" align="center">FACTFILE</td></tr>
<tr>
<td>

Tribe: JUDAH

Father: JESSE

Brothers: ELIAB, ABINADAB, SHIMA, NETHANEEL, RADDAI, OZEM (1 SAMUEL 16:10 MENTIONS SEVEN BROTHERS; 1 CHRONICLES 2:13–15 NAMES ONLY SIX)

</td>
<td>

Sisters: ZERUIAH, ABIGAIL

Wives: MICHAL, AHINOAM, ABIGAIL, MAACAH, BATHSHEBA AND OTHER WIVES AND CONCUBINES

Sons: AMNON, ABSALOM, ADONIJAH AND OTHERS

Daughters: TAMAR AND OTHERS

</td>
</tr>
</table>

David is one of the key figures in the Old Testament, not just for what he was and what he did but for what he came to represent in Judaism and Christianity. Matthew makes David pivotal in his genealogy of Jesus (1:17).

KEY EPISODES IN THE LIFE OF DAVID

HIS ANOINTING AS KING

God sends Samuel to Bethlehem, to anoint one of Jesse's sons king. God directs Samuel to anoint David, the youngest son (1 Samuel 16).

✦

DAVID ENTERS SAUL'S SERVICE AND KILLS GOLIATH

Saul is, however, unaware of David's anointing. Troubled by an evil spirit, he summons David to play the harp for him. David also becomes his armour-bearer. David kills the Philistine giant Goliath, but becomes so popular that he arouses Saul's jealousy (18). In spite of this, David is given Saul's daughter Michal as a wife.

✦

SAUL TRIES TO KILL DAVID

On more than one occasion Saul tries to kill David. David is forced to flee for his life; on two occasions he even flees to the Philistines for safety. Although David twice has the chance to kill Saul, he respects God's anointed king and each time he spares Saul's life. David is not safe until Saul, defeated by the Philistines, commits suicide.

✦

DAVID KING OF JUDAH

On Saul's death, David is anointed king by the men of Judah, his own tribe, while the rest of Israel chooses Saul's son Ishbosheth to be their king (2 Samuel 2). David reigns in the town of Hebron for seven and a half years.

✦

DAVID KING OF A UNITED ISRAEL

After a period of civil war between Judah and the rest of Israel, Ishbosheth is murdered. The men of Israel invite David to be their king too (2 Samuel 5). Having taken Jerusalem and its fortress Zion from the Jebusites, David transfers his capital from Hebron to Jerusalem, where he reigns for a further 33 years. He brings the ark of the Covenant to Jerusalem, and intends to build a temple for it, but through Nathan the prophet, God tells David that it is not he but his son who will build the temple.

✦

DAVID AND BATHSHEBA

One day David, out on the roof of the palace, sees a beautiful woman, Bathsheba, bathing. She is the wife of one of David's soldiers, Uriah the Hittite. They commit adultery and Bathsheba becomes pregnant (2 Samuel 11). David arranges for Uriah to die in battle; he then marries Bathsheba, but their child dies. However, Bathsheba bears David four more sons, one of whom is Solomon, the next king of Israel. Psalm 51 was written by David when he was upbraided by the prophet Nathan for taking Uriah's wife.

✦

ABSALOM'S REBELLION

David's third son Absalom, who had fallen out with his father over the murder of his half-brother Amnon but been reconciled with him again, sets himself up as king at Hebron. David flees from Jerusalem. But in a great battle, Absalom's army is utterly defeated by David's forces and Absalom is killed, contrary to David's orders. David mourns the death of his son.

TENSIONS BETWEEN JUDAH AND ISRAEL

The argument over who should escort David back to Jerusalem and the brief rebellion led by the Benjaminite Sheba (2 Samuel 19–20) shows the deep divide between David's tribe of Judah and the other tribes of Israel. These tensions underlie the division of the kingdom after the death of Solomon.

✦

SOLOMON ANOINTED KING

At the end of David's reign, his oldest remaining son Adonijah claims the kingship. But Bathsheba reminds David that he promised that Solomon was to be king after him. Solomon is anointed king by the priest Zadok and the prophet Nathan (1 Kings 1:45), and after reigning for 40 years, David dies.

David's character

Although David is seen as a great king and national hero, the Bible writers do not gloss over his faults. He is brave, loyal (even to Saul, who was trying to kill him), a loving and forgiving father (even to Absalom, who rebelled against him), a good friend, a man of action, a just ruler, a gifted musician and poet, and faithful to God. But he is also an adulterer and murderer (Bathsheba and Uriah), and he harbours grudges: after accepting Shimei's curses as coming from God (2 Samuel 16) and promising him that his life would be spared (19:23), on his death-bed he instructs Solomon to put Shimei to death (1 Kings 2:9).

DAVID'S SIGNIFICANCE

Jesus is called the 'Son of David' eight times in the gospels. Parallels are explicitly made between the kingship of David and the kingship of Jesus: when the angel Gabriel announces to Mary that she will bear a son, he tells her that:

'the Lord God shall give unto him the throne of his father David: And he shall reign over the house of Jacob for ever'
(Luke 1:32–33).

THE PSALMS

King David and King Solomon
Led merry, merry lives,
With many, many lady friends
And many, many wives;
But when old age crept over them,
With many, many qualms,
King Solomon wrote the Proverbs
And King David wrote the Psalms.
(James Ball Naylor)

WHO WROTE THE PSALMS?

The Psalms are often referred to as the 'Psalms of David', but David didn't write all of them. (Indeed, some scholars question whether he actually wrote any of them.) In the Book of Psalms itself, only 73 psalms are attributed to David.

Other psalms are attributed to Asaph (psalms 50, 73 to 83), to the sons of Korah (42, 44 to 49, 84, 85, 87 and 88), to King Solomon (72 and 127), to Heman (also 88), to Ethan (89) and to Moses (90). Some psalms have no attribution at all.

Asaph was one of the singers and instrumentalists in the tent of the Ark of the Covenant (1 Chronicles 16). The sons of Korah were probably a guild of musicians. Asaph and Korah were both descendants of Levi.

David was a talented harpist, who played for King Saul when he was troubled by an evil spirit (1 Samuel 16). In 2 Samuel 23:1, David is referred to as the 'sweet psalmist of Israel'. One ancient tradition says that he wrote 4,050 psalms!

The Book of Psalms is also known as the Psalter. The English word 'psalter' comes via Latin from Greek *psalterion*, a stringed musical instrument.

FACTFILE

The Book of Psalms is a compilation of several earlier collections of religious songs. The psalms were probably written between 1000BC and 200BC.

✳

In some groups of psalms, e.g. the first 41 psalms, God is generally addressed as 'Yahweh', in other groups, e.g. 42 to 83, as 'Elohim'.

✳

The shortest psalm is psalm 117 (consisting of only 2 verses). The longest psalm is psalm 119 (with 176 verses).

✳

Psalm 119 is divided into 22 sections of 8 verses, each section being headed by a letter of the Hebrew alphabet in alphabetical order.

✳

In its Hebrew form, Psalm 119 is an acrostic. The first word in each of the eight verses in each section begins with the letter heading that section.

✳

Other psalms are acrostics or have acrostic sections, e.g. 25, 34, 37, 111, 112, 145.

✳

Psalm 103 contains the middle two verses of the Bible (verses 1–2):
BLESS THE LORD, O MY SOUL: AND ALL THAT IS WITHIN ME, BLESS HIS HOLY NAME. BLESS THE LORD, O MY SOUL, AND FORGET NOT ALL HIS BENEFITS.

✳

Some psalms occur twice, e.g. Psalm 14 is the same as Psalm 53, Psalm 70 is a repeat of Psalm 40:13-17.

✳

Psalm 104 has parallels with the Hymn to the Sun of the Pharaoh Akhenaten.

✳

The 8th, 15th, 21st and 31st verses of Psalm 107 are identical.

✳

Each verse of Psalm 136 ends in the same phrase.

✳

Because all the major themes of the Bible story can be found in it, the Book of Psalms is sometimes called 'the Bible within the Bible'. Martin Luther called Psalms 'the Bible in miniature'.

✳

The numbering of the psalms varies slightly in different versions of the Bible. (The numbering here follows the King James Version.)

✳

The Book of Psalms ends with 'Praise ye the Lord'.

WHAT IS IN THE BOOK OF PSALMS?

The Book of Psalms has been the main hymn book of Judaism and Christianity. The apostle Paul writes of the early church singing 'psalms and hymns and spiritual songs' (Colossians 3:16). The subject matter of the Psalms covers the whole gamut of human experience:

> *some psalms are songs of praise and thanksgiving to God* (e.g. Psalms 98, 100, 150)
> ❖ *some contain moral teaching and exhortation* (e.g. Psalms 1, 37) ❖ *some express*
> *penitence for wrongdoing* (Psalms 6, 32, 38, 51) ❖ *some recount the story of the Israelites*
> *and relationship with God* (e.g. Psalms 78, 105–107) ❖ *some are laments* (e.g. Psalms 3,
> 13, 74, 79) ❖ *some are seen as foretelling the Messiah* (e.g. Psalms 2, 8, 16).

From the Latin words with which they begin in the Vulgate, Psalm 51 is known as the 'Miserere' and Psalm 130 as 'De profundis'.

> *Some of the hundred and fifty lyrics which make up the psalter*
> *surpass the best products of religious literature anywhere. Others*
> *are as uninspired as many of our hymns today.*
> William Neil

The Pentateuch of David

In the Hebrew Bible (and some Christian Bibles), the psalms are divided into five groups: 1–41; 42–72; 73–89; 90–106; 107–150. The end of each group is indicated by the word 'Amen'. Each of these groups of psalms has been associated in Jewish and Christian theology with the Pentateuch (the first five books of the Bible):

- GENESIS: psalms 1–41 (both are said to encapsulate the whole Bible)
- EXODUS psalms 42–72 (suffering and redemption)
- LEVITICUS: psalms 73–89 (holiness)
- NUMBERS: psalms 90–106 (wandering and rest)
- DEUTERONOMY: psalms 107–150 (gathering and praise)

For this reason the Book of Psalms is sometimes called the 'Pentateuch of David'.

DAVID THE PROPHET

Although the Book of Psalms is a book of religious songs, it is also seen by Jews and Christians as a book of prophecy, and David is considered to be among the prophets. Jesus himself teaches that the psalms speak about him:

And he said unto them, These are the words which I spake unto you, while I was yet with you, that all things must be fulfilled, which were written in the law of Moses, and in the prophets, and in the psalms, concerning me. (Luke 24:44)

Jesus quotes from the Psalms more often than from any other book of the Old Testament. For example, his words:

The stone which the builders rejected is become the head of the corner: This was the Lord's doing, and it is marvellous in our eyes (Mark 12:10–11)

are taken from Psalm 118. And when Jesus enters Jerusalem, the words of the crowd:

Hosanna; Blessed is he that cometh in the name of the Lord (Mark 1:9)

are also quoting this psalm.

On the Day of Pentecost, Peter quotes from the prophet Joel and from the Psalms, referring to David as a prophet (Acts 2:29–30). In this, the first Christian sermon of the new church, Peter quotes

from three psalms: Psalm 16 (Acts 2:25–28), Psalm 132 (Acts 2:30), and Psalm 110 (Acts 2:34–35).

MY GOD, WHY HAVE YOU FORSAKEN ME? Jesus cries to God from the cross:

Eli, Eli, lama sabachthani? that is to say, My God, my God, why hast thou forsaken me? (Matthew 27:46)

These are the opening words of Psalm 22.

PSALM 23

The best-known psalm is surely Psalm 23:

> *The LORD is my shepherd; I shall not want.*
> *He maketh me to lie down in green pastures: he leadeth me beside the*
> *still waters.*
> *He restoreth my soul: he leadeth me in the paths of righteousness for his*
> *name's sake.*
> *Yea, though I walk through the valley of the shadow of death, I will fear no*
> *evil: for thou art with me; thy rod and thy staff they comfort me.*
> *Thou preparest a table before me in the presence of mine enemies: thou*
> *anointest my head with oil; my cup runneth over.*
> *Surely goodness and mercy shall follow me all the days of my life: and I will*
> *dwell in the house of the LORD for ever.*

Several beautiful hymns have been based on this psalm, such as Henry Williams Baker's *The King of Love my Shepherd is* and Isaac Watts' three hymns *My Shepherd will supply my need, My shepherd is the living Lord* and *The Lord my shepherd is.*

Isaac Watts (1674–1748) wrote new versions of all the psalms, though many are not well known nowadays. Among other well-known hymns based on the psalms are Watts' *Jesus shall reign where'er the sun* (based on Psalm 72) and *O God our help in ages past* (based on Psalm 90), Henry Francis Lyle's *Praise my soul, the King of Heaven* (based on Psalm 103) and Sir Robert Grant's *O worship the King, all glorious above* (based on Psalm 104).

According to William of Malmesbury, King Alfred the Great (849–901) was working on an English translation of the psalms at the time of his death.

THE CURSING PSALMS

Of particular difficulty for many people are the psalms known as the cursing psalms or imprecatory psalms. These are psalms that call down God's wrath on God's enemies or Israel's enemies with a degree of delight and hostility that seems inappropriate in religious songs. Take, for example, Psalm 137: 8–9:

O daughter of Babylon, who art to be destroyed; happy shall he be, that rewardeth thee as thou hast served us. Happy shall he be, that taketh and dasheth thy little ones against the stones.

In a similar vein, there is Psalm 109: 8–15:

Let his days be few; and let another take his office. Let his children be fatherless, and his wife a widow. Let his children be continually vagabonds, and beg: let them seek their bread also out of their desolate places. Let the extortioner catch all that he hath; and let the strangers spoil his labour. Let there be none to extend mercy unto him: neither let there be any to favour his fatherless children. Let his posterity be cut off; and in the generation following let their name be blotted out. Let the iniquity of his fathers be remembered with the Lord; and let not the sin of his mother be blotted out. Let them be before the Lord continually, that he may cut off the memory of them from the earth.

Other psalms that may be included among the imprecatory psalms (lists vary) are Psalms 5, 11, 35, 52, 58, 64, 69, 70, 83 and 140.

It is said that during the Middle Ages Psalm 109 was sometimes recited by dying men in a final death-bed attempt to bring about the death and destruction of their most hated enemies. Not perhaps a very Christian attitude!

Psalm 46: the Shakespeare psalm

The 46th word of Psalm 46 is 'shake', and the word 46 from the end is 'spear'. And at the time the King James Bible was being finally revised, the playwright William Shakespeare (born 1564) would have been 46 years old.

Royal Psalms

Ten psalms (numbers 2, 18, 20, 21, 28, 45, 61, 63, 72, 89, 101, 110 and 132) are known as the Royal Psalms. They celebrate aspects of the king's relationship with God.

WISDOM PSALMS

Some ten or so psalms (lists vary but include some of Psalms 1, 37, 49, 73, 112, 127, 128 and 133) are known as the Wisdom Psalms. The Wisdom Psalms look at life, morality, happiness and so on, in much the same way as the Wisdom literature such as Proverbs and Ecclesiastes.

PSALMS 151 TO 155

If you look for Psalm 151 in a Bible, the chances are you won't find it. But there is a 151st psalm, and it is included in some Bibles, such as the *New Revised Standard Version.* Psalm 151 is not found in the Hebrew Bible but was included in the Greek version known as the Septuagint. It is not included in the canon by Protestants or Roman Catholics, but it is accepted as canonical by some Orthodox churches. The psalm is ascribed to David, and its title claims that it was written by him after he killed the Philistine giant Goliath.

A further four psalms, 152 to 155, are found in some ancient translations of the Bible.

SOLOMON IN ALL HIS GLORY

FACTFILE

Father: DAVID
Mother: BATHSHEBA
Also named JEDIDIAH (2
SAMUEL 12:25), WHICH MEANS
'LOVED BY GOD'
*Ruled over Israel from
c.970 to 930BC.*

THE LIFE OF SOLOMON

SOLOMON ASKS FOR WISDOM

One night the Lord appears to Solomon in a dream and tells him he can ask for anything he wants. Solomon asks for 'an understanding heart' so that he can 'discern between good and bad' and judge wisely (1 Kings 3:9). God grants this, and because Solomon has not asked for a long life or great wealth, God grants him these too.

Solomon's wisdom and knowledge was said to be even greater than that of the wise men of the east and the wise men of Egypt.

✦

TWO PROSTITUTES AND A BABY

Two prostitutes come to Solomon, arguing over a baby (1 Kings 3). They both have had babies, but one has died. Both women claim the remaining baby is theirs. To settle the matter, Solomon suggests cutting the baby in two, each to take one half. One woman agrees; the other says she would rather her rival kept the baby than that it be cut up and killed. Solomon decrees that it is the second prostitute who is the baby's real mother. And the whole country is amazed at the king's wisdom and discernment.

✦

SOLOMON'S KINGDOM

Solomon ruled over territory stretching from the river Euphrates (now in Iraq) to the Mediterranean coast, and south to the Egyptian border.

✦

THE TEMPLE

In the fourth year of Solomon's reign, work begins on the Temple in Jerusalem, using a workforce of over 180,000 men. The Temple is 60 cubits long, 20 cubits wide and 30 cubits high (= 88 × 30 × 44 feet or 27 × 9 × 13.5 metres) and takes seven years to build.

THE QUEEN OF SHEBA

Hearing of Solomon's wisdom, the Queen of Sheba (modern Yemen) travels to Jerusalem to see him and test him with hard questions (1 Kings 10). There isn't a single question that Solomon is unable to answer. It is agreed by many scholars that the Queen's visit may have been in the context of a trade mission.

Solomon's wives and concubines

Solomon has 700 wives and 300 concubines. Many are not Israelites, and when they come to Jerusalem they bring their own religions with them. By the time Solomon has reached old age, he has been led astray by his wives into the worship of their gods. For this apostasy, God tells Solomon that his son will lose the kingdom, retaining only one tribe to rule over (1 Kings 11:13). Through the prophet Ahijah, God promises Jeroboam, one of Solomon's officials, that he will become king of ten tribes (11:30–32). And after Solomon's death the northern tribes do revolt against his son Rehoboam, and the kingdom of Israel splits into a northern kingdom of Israel and a southern kingdom of Judah.

Although according to the prophecy Rehoboam will retain the loyalty of only one tribe, Judah, it is clear from 1 Kings 12:21 that the tribe of Benjamin also remained loyal to him. In 1 Chronicles 14, King Asa of Judah has almost as many soldiers from the tribe of Benjamin as he has from the tribe of Judah.

In the gospels, Jesus' descent from David is traced by Matthew through Solomon and Rehoboam but by Luke though Solomon's brother Nathan, also a son of Bathsheba.

WISDOM FROM PROVERBS AND ECCLESIASTES

The Book of Proverbs begins: 'The proverbs of Solomon, the son of David, king of Israel'. Solomon is said to have written 3,000 proverbs and 1,005 songs (1 Kings 4:32). However, the book contains more than the proverbs of Solomon, since chapter 10 is headed 'the proverbs of Solomon' and chapter 25 begins 'these are also proverbs of Solomon'. Other sections, such as the 'words of the wise' beginning at 22:17, are by other writers. Ecclesiastes begins with 'The words of the Preacher, the son of David, king in Jerusalem', but nowhere is it actually said that the writer is Solomon.

Works of this sort are known as 'wisdom literature'.

WISE WORDS FROM THE PROVERBS

Trust in the LORD with all thine heart; and lean not unto thine own understanding.

The fear of the LORD is the beginning of wisdom: and the knowledge of the holy is understanding.

❖

Hatred stirreth up strifes: but love covereth all sins.

As vinegar to the teeth, and as smoke to the eyes, so is the sluggard to them that send him.

❖

Whoso loveth instruction loveth knowledge: but he that hateth reproof is brutish.

When pride cometh, then cometh shame: but with the lowly is wisdom.

❖

As a jewel of gold in a swine's snout, so is a fair woman which is without discretion.

❖

A man shall be commended according to his wisdom: but he that is of a perverse heart shall be despised.

❖

The way of a fool is right in his own eyes: but he that hearkeneth unto counsel is wise.

❖

He that walketh with wise men shall be wise: but a companion of fools shall be destroyed.

Righteousness exalteth a nation: but sin is
a reproach to any people.

❖

A soft answer turneth away wrath: but
grievous words stir up anger.

❖

Better is little with the fear of the LORD
than great treasure and trouble therewith.

❖

A merry heart doeth good like a medicine:
but a broken spirit drieth the bones.
He also that is slothful in his work is
brother to him that is a great waster.

❖

Whoso findeth a wife findeth a good
thing, and obtaineth favour of the LORD.

Wine is a mocker, strong drink is raging:
and whosoever is deceived thereby is
not wise.

❖

He that loveth pleasure shall be a poor
man: he that loveth wine and oil shall
not be rich.

❖

It is better to dwell in the wilderness, than
with a contentious and an angry woman.

❖

A fool uttereth all his mind: but a wise
man keepeth it in till afterwards.

❖

Where there is no vision, the people perish:
but he that keepeth the law, happy is he.

Wise words from Ecclesiastes

◆ Vanity of vanities, saith the Preacher, vanity of vanities; all is vanity.

◆ To every thing there is a season, and a time to every purpose under the heaven.

◆ A good name is better than precious ointment.

◆ It is better to hear the rebuke of the wise, than for a man to hear the song of fools.

◆ He that loveth silver shall not be satisfied with silver.

◆ Be not hasty in thy spirit to be angry: for anger resteth in the bosom of fools.

◆ Fear God, and keep his commandments: for this is the whole duty of man.

THE SONG OF SOLOMON

According to 1 Kings 4:32, King Solomon wrote 1,005 songs, and the first verse of the Song of Solomon says that of all of them this was the 'song of songs', his very best. It is, however, not one song, but a series of love poems or songs addressed by a man and a woman to one another, along with some short passages spoken by others. Whether or not the poems were written by Solomon, he is mentioned several times in the book, and the reference to 'threescore queens and fourscore concubines' (6:8) might also make one think of a king like Solomon – though he had 700 wives and 300 concubines!

The Song of Solomon is one of the two books in the Bible in which there is no mention of God (Esther is the other).

Interpreting the poems allegorically rather than literally, Jewish rabbis saw in the love between the man and the woman an image of the love between God and Israel. Christian teaching has equated the lovers with Christ and either the Church, the soul of the believer or the Virgin Mary.

There are many beautiful phrases and images in the Song of Solomon:
- ✲ *Many waters cannot quench love, nor can the floods drown it.*
- ✲ *Love is strong as death.*
- ✲ *Thy love is better than wine.*
- ✲ *As the lily among thorns, so is my love among the daughters.*
- ✲ *As the apple tree among the trees of the wood, so is my beloved among the sons.*
- ✲ *Thy lips are like a thread of scarlet.*

Some of the images are a little surprising:

- ✲ *Thy hair is as a flock of goats that appear from mount Gilead.*
- ✲ *Thy teeth are like a flock of sheep that are even shorn, which came up from the washing.*

ESTHER

Esther and the Song of Solomon are the only books in the Bible in which God is not mentioned. There are additions to Esther in the Apocrypha, where God *is* mentioned.

Esther is a Jewish girl who becomes the wife of King Ahasuerus of Persia. Ahasuerus' chief official, Haman, plots to have all the Jews in the Persian empire murdered. Risking her life, because it is forbidden to approach the king unless summoned by him, Esther goes to Ahasuerus and invites him and Haman to a banquet. At a second banquet, Esther exposes Haman's plot and he is hanged on gallows he had planned to have Esther's uncle hanged on. The Jews are permitted to protect themselves.

The Feast of Purim is celebrated in memory of these events, as Haman had cast lots (purim) to decide the day on which to have the Jews murdered.

JOB

The theme of this book is the problem of why bad things happen to good people. Job is a wealthy, good and pious man. However, Satan suggests to God that Job only loves God because God has been good to him: take away all Job has and he would curse God. God gives Satan permission to test Job: in a series of blows, he loses his family, his wealth  and his health. Three friends come to comfort him, but in a long discussion on why Job has suffered in this way they offer little comfort, trying to persuade Job that he must have brought the misfortunes on himself by some wrongdoing. In the end, God himself appears, condemns Job's friends for their false arguments, asserts his omnipotence and restores Job's fortunes.

'Job's comforter' has become a proverbial expression for someone whose attempts to offer comfort simply make things worse. Job's patient acceptance of his suffering has also given rise to the expression 'the patience of Job'.

ISRAEL AND JUDAH

❖ The history of Israel and Judah is written in 1 &
2 Kings and 1 & 2 Chronicles.

❖ 1 Kings begins with the death of David, and
2 Kings ends with the fall of Jerusalem to the
Babylonians and the destruction of the Temple
in 586BC.

❖ 1 Chronicles begins with Adam, and 2 Chronicles
ends with the fall of Babylon to the Persians in
539BC and the decree of the Persian king Cyrus
that the Jews should return to Jerusalem to rebuild
the Temple.

❖ The history of Jerusalem and Judah continues in
the books of Ezra and Nehemiah.

THE KINGS OF ISRAEL (930–722BC)

JEROBOAM I *(22 years)* ♦ NADAB *(2 years)* ♦ BAASHA *(24 years)* ♦ ELAH
(2 years) ♦ ZIMRI *(7 days)* ♦ OMRI *(12 years)* ♦ AHAB *(22 years)*
♦ AHAZIAH *(2 years)* ♦ JEHORAM *(12 years)* ♦ JEHU *(28 years)* ♦ JEHOAHAZ
(17 years) ♦ JEHOASH *(16 years)* ♦ JEROBOAM II *(41 years)* ♦ ZECHARIAH
(6 months) ♦ SHALLUM *(1 month)* ♦ MENAHEM *(17 years)* ♦ PEKAHIAH
(2 years) ♦ PEKAH *(20 years)* ♦ HOSHEA *(9 years)*

Israel fell to the Assyrians in 722BC.

THE KINGS (AND QUEEN) OF JUDAH (930–586BC)

REHOBOAM *(17 years)* ♦ ABIJAM *(3 years)* ♦ ASA *(41 years)* ♦ JEHOSHAPHAT
(25 years) ♦ JEHORAM *(8 years)* ♦ AHAZIAH *(1 year)* ♦ QUEEN ATHALIAH
(6 years) ♦ JOASH *(40 years)* ♦ AMAZIAH *(29 years)* ♦ AZARIAH *(52 years)*
♦ JOTHAM *(16 years)* ♦ AHAZ *(16 years)* ♦ HEZEKIAH *(29 years)*
♦ MANASSEH *(55 years)* ♦ AMON *(2 years)* ♦ JOSIAH *(31 years)*
♦ JEHOAHAZ *(3 months)* ♦ JEHOIAKIM *(11 years)* ♦ JEHOIACHIN *(3 months)*
♦ ZEDEKIAH *(11 years)*

Judah fell to the Babylonians in 586BC.

Athaliah was the only queen to rule in Israel or Judah.

Some reigns overlapped. Some of the short reigns ended with
assassination.

The history in these books is history from a religious viewpoint. Israel and Judah and their kings are assessed, not in terms of their secular success, but in terms of their adherence to the Law of God. Both nations, and most kings, arouse God's anger with repeated apostasy.

JEROBOAM

Fearing that if the people of Israel go back to Jerusalem to worship, he will lose their loyalty, Jeroboam sets up golden calf idols in Dan (in the north of Israel) and Bethel (in the south). For this apostasy, the kingship is taken from his family (1 Kings 14:14).

OMRI

Omri buys the hill of Samaria, fortifies it, builds a town there, and makes it the capital of Israel. For the next two centuries, Israel is known to the Assyrians as the 'land of Omri'. However, the Bible's main concern is that he 'wrought evil in the eyes of the LORD, and did worse than all that were before him' (1 Kings 16:25).

AHAB AND JEZEBEL

Omri's son Ahab marries Jezebel, daughter of the king of Tyre and Sidon, and builds a temple to Jezebel's god Baal in Samaria. Ahab and Jezebel come into conflict with the prophet Elijah, who challenges the prophets of Baal to a contest. They and he will each build an altar and pray to their god to set alight the wood on it. The prophets of Baal dance and pray, but in vain. Then it's Elijah's turn: to make things harder, he even has his altar soaked with water. When Elijah prays, God sends down fire and burns up the whole altar. The prophets of Baal are put to death.

THE FALL OF ISRAEL

After a three-year siege, Samaria falls to the Assyrians in 722BC. The people of Israel (or a large number of them) are deported to the Assyrian empire: because of their failure to heed the prophets God has sent, 'the Lord was very angry with Israel, and removed them out of his sight' (2 Kings 17:18). The Israelites are replaced by non-Israelite immigrants, and never return.

Many theories and legends have developed regarding the 'lost tribes' of Israel and what happened to them after they were taken to Assyria. There are several ethnic groups throughout the world who claim descent from one or more of these tribes, such as the Falashas of Ethiopia and the Chiang Min of China. British Israelites believe that the Anglo-Saxon and Celtic peoples are descended from the Israelites.

JOSIAH

During the reign of Josiah, while the Temple is being repaired, a 'book of the law of the Lord given by Moses' is discovered. Many scholars believe that this book was, or contained, the Book of Deuteronomy. Josiah reads the book to the people and they make a covenant to obey the law of God.

THE FALL OF JUDAH

As with Israel, so with Judah. For their sins and their apostasy, God decides to 'cast them out from his presence' (2 Kings 24:20). Judah rebels against the Babylonians: Jerusalem falls in 597BC, and after a further rebellion the city is destroyed in 586BC.

THE RETURN TO JERUSALEM

In 539BC, the Persians conquer Babylon. Prompted by God, Cyrus orders the Jews to return to Jerusalem to rebuild the temple (Ezra 1). Some years later, Ezra is sent by Artaxerxes to help the people organize their religious life correctly (Ezra 7), and then Nehemiah is sent to rebuild the city walls (Nehemiah 2) .

KINGS OF ASSYRIA, BABYLONIA AND PERSIA

Tiglath-pileser III	also Tilgath-pilneser; Assyrian king 745–727BC; aided King Ahaz of Judah against King Pekah of Israel (2 Kings 16)
Shalmaneser	Shalmaneser V, king of Assyria from 727 to 722BC; besieged Samaria for three years (2 Kings 17)
Sargon	king of Assyria 722–705BC; completed the capture of Samaria 722BC
Sennacherib	king of Assyria 705–681BC; unsuccessfully invaded Judah during the reign of Hezekiah (2 Kings 18–19)
Esarhaddon	son of Sennacherib; king of Assyria 681–669BC; took King Manasseh of Judah captive (2 Chronicles 33:11)
Ashurbanipal	king of Assyria (c.669–627BC); probably the Asnappar of Ezra 4:10
Nebuchadnezzar	Nebuchadnezzar (or Nebuchadrezzar) II; king of Babylon 605–562BC; the king who captured and destroyed Jerusalem in 586BC, and the king whom Daniel and his friends served
Evil-merodach	son of Nebuchadnezzar; king 562–560BC
Belshazzar	the last king of Babylon, according to the Book of Daniel; the king who saw the writing on the wall; ruled 539BC
Cyrus	Cyrus II, Persian king (c.559–530BC); conquered Babylonia in 539BC; sent the Jews back to Jerusalem to rebuild the temple
Darius	❶ according to the Book of Daniel, 'Darius the Mede' was the Persian king who conquered Babylon in 539BC; there was no Darius on the Persian throne at this time, and it was Cyrus who captured Babylon ❷ Darius I (521–486BC), the Persian king who allowed work on the Temple to restart (Ezra 6)
Ahasuerus	the Persian king in the Book of Esther; almost certainly Xerxes I, king of Persia from 485 to 465BC
Artaxerxes	❶ Artaxerxes I (464–424BC), the Persian king who sent Ezra and Nehemiah to Jerusalem ❷ Artaxerxes II, king of Persia from 404 to 359BC

THE PROPHETS

THE BOOKS OF THE PROPHETS IN THEIR BIBLICAL ORDER

Isaiah ♦ Jeremiah ♦ Ezekiel ♦ Daniel ♦ Hosea ♦ Joel ♦ Amos ♦ Obadiah ♦ Jonah ♦ Micah ♦ Nahum ♦ Habakkuk ♦ Zephaniah ♦ Haggai ♦ Zechariah ♦ Malachi

Other prophets, such as Samuel, Nathan, Elijah and Elisha, speak on God's behalf throughout the historical books of the Bible. Abraham was the first prophet (Genesis 20:7). Moses was not only the Israelite leader on the journey to Canaan, but also a prophet (Deuteronomy 34:10). King David is also considered a prophet (Acts 2:29–30).

FOUR PROPHETESSES ARE MENTIONED IN THE OLD TESTAMENT:

Deborah ♦ Huldah ♦ Miriam ♦ Noadiah (a false prophetess)

Isaiah's wife is also referred to as 'the prophetess' (Isaiah 8:3).

According to Jewish scholars, there have been 48 prophets and seven prophetesses.

Prophets and seers

Beforetime in Israel, when a man went to inquire of God, thus he spake, Come, and let us go to the seer: for he that is now called a Prophet was beforetime called a Seer' (1 Samuel 9:9). Some prophets acted alone, while others belonged to communities: 'And when they came thither to the hill, behold, a company of prophets met him (1 Samuel 10:10).

False prophets and their punishment

Thus saith the LORD concerning the prophets that prophesy in my name, and I sent them not, yet they say, Sword and famine shall not be in this land; By sword and famine shall those prophets be consumed (Jeremiah 14:15).

How to recognize a false prophet

When a prophet speaketh in the name of the LORD, if the thing follow not, nor come to pass, that is the thing which the LORD hath not spoken, but the prophet hath spoken it presumptuously: thou shalt not be afraid of him (Deuteronomy 18:22).

✳ In the Jewish Bible, Daniel is not listed among the Prophets but among the Writings. But Jesus refers to him as a prophet (Matthew 24.15), and for many Christians Daniel is an important prophetic book.

✳ The Book of Lamentations was traditionally attributed to Jeremiah, but there is no biblical warrant for this beyond a tenuous connection with Jeremiah's lament for King Josiah (2 Chronicles 35:25). Because of his presumed authorship of Lamentations, Jeremiah is often depicted in art as the 'weeping prophet'. A 'jeremiad' is a long lamentation or complaint.

Jeremiah had a secretary, Baruch (Jeremiah 32:12–16). There is a Book of Baruch in the Apocrypha, chapter 6 of which is a letter supposedly written by Jeremiah to Jews who were about to be taken captive to Babylon.

THE PROPHETS IN HISTORICAL ORDER

(Some of the following dates are by no means certain. For example, Joel has been placed as early as the 9th century and as late as the 4th century BC.)

JOEL *(8th century BC)* ♦ AMOS *(8th century BC)* ♦ JONAH *(8th century BC)* ♦ HOSEA *(8th century BC)* ♦ ISAIAH *(8th century BC)* ♦ MICAH *(8th to 7th century BC)* ♦ NAHUM *(7th century BC)* ♦ ZEPHANIAH *(7th century BC)* ♦ JEREMIAH *(7th to 6th century BC)* ♦ HABAKKUK *(7th century BC)* ♦ DANIEL *(7th to 6th century BC)* ♦ EZEKIEL *(6th century BC)* ♦ OBADIAH *(6th century BC)* ♦ HAGGAI *(6th century BC)* ♦ ZECHARIAH *(6th century BC)* ♦ MALACHI *(5th century BC)*

Isaiah: one prophet or three?

Many scholars see the Book of Isaiah as the work of more than one prophet. The book is often separated into three parts: chapters 1–39 (First Isaiah), 40–55 (Second Isaiah) and 56–66 (Third Isaiah).

According to Jewish tradition, prophecy ended with Malachi.
Malachi means 'my messenger'. It is not certain whether this is the prophet's actual name.
According to one tradition, 'Malachi' was Ezra, the scribe sent to Jerusalem by Artaxerxes.

THE MESSAGE OF THE PROPHETS

prophesy, your old men shall dream dreams, your young men shall see visions.' (2:28)

✦ AMOS

Describes God's judgement on Israel's neighbours, and on Israel itself for its social injustice and its shallow worship; God's impending judgment is shown in five visions; ends with a picture of a restored Israel.

'Let judgment run down as waters, and righteousness as a mighty stream.' (5:24)

✦ HOSEA

Hosea's faithless wife represents a faithless Israel who has gone after other gods; Israel will be punished, but in the end, God's love for his people will prevail.

'I desired mercy, and not sacrifice; and the knowledge of God more than burnt offerings.' (6:6) *'They have sown the wind, and they shall reap the whirlwind.'* (8:7)

✦ JOEL

Describes a plague of locusts and a terrible drought, events Joel sees as a sign of the coming of the Day of the Lord; the people are called to repent; the nations will be judged and Judah will be restored.

'I will pour out my spirit upon all flesh; and your sons and your daughters shall

✦ MICAH

Judah will be punished for its corruption, social injustice and false relgious practices, but there is an expectation that God will be merciful.

'What doth the Lord require of thee, but to do justly, and to love mercy, and to walk humbly with thy God?' (6:8)

✦ ISAIAH

Begins with a condemnation of the sins of Jerusalem and warning of punishment to come; the coming of Immanuel; punishment of the nations, and of Israel and Judah, but with a promise of hope.

(Chapters 40–55) Comforts the Jewish exiles in Babylon, with a promise of a judgement on Babylon and the restoration of Jerusalem; describes the 'suffering servant' who is punished for our sins.

(Chapters 56–66) Condemns sin and idolatry, and looks forward to a new Jerusalem.

'Behold, a virgin shall conceive, and bear a son, and shall call his name Immanuel.'
(7:14)

✳

'For unto us a child is born, unto us a son is given: and the government shall be upon his shoulder: and his name shall be called Wonderful, Counseller, The Mighty God, The Everlasting Father, The Prince of Peace. Of the increase of his government and peace there shall be no end, upon the throne of David, and upon his kingdom, to order it, and to establish it with judgment and with justice from henceforth even for ever.' (9:6–7)

✳

'He was wounded for our transgressions, he was bruised for our iniquities: the chastisement of our peace was upon him; and with his stripes we are healed. All we like sheep have gone astray; we have turned every one to his own way; and the Lord hath laid on him the iniquity of us all.' (53:5–6)

✳

'Is not this the fast that I have chosen? To loose the bands of wickedness, to undo the heavy burdens, and to let the oppressed go free, and that ye break every yoke? Is it not to deal thy bread to the hungry, and that thou bring the poor that are cast out to thy house? When thou seest the naked, that thou cover him; and that thou hide not thyself from thine own flesh?' (58:6–7)

To the Gentiles, Joel said:
'Prepare war. Beat your plowshares into swords, and your pruninghooks into spears' (3:9–10).
Visualizing a future time of peace, Micah (4:3) and Isaiah (2:4) turn these words the other way round:
'They shall beat their swords into plowshares, and their spears into pruninghooks: nation shall not lift up a sword against nation, neither shall they learn war any more.'

✦ **NAHUM**

Celebrates the impending fall of Nineveh and Assyria, an act of God which will save from Judah from the Assyrians.

✦ **ZEPHANIAH**

Attacks the worship of other gods, and predicts an impending Day of the Lord, 'a day of wrath, a day of trouble and distress' (1:15). The nations will be judged, and God's people will prosper again.

✦ **JEREMIAH**

Warns against idolatry and immorality, and calls Judah and Israel to repent; punishment and restoration.

✦ **HABAKKUK**

The prophet asks God why he allows evil and injustice to go unpunished. God replies that he will use the Babylonians to punish wrongdoing. But they are evil too, complains the prophet. God says that their pride will be their downfall.

✦ **EZEKIEL**

Condemns the sins of Israel and Judah; warns of judgement on the nations; describes the restoration of Jerusalem and the Temple.

✦ **OBADIAH**

God will judge the nations; Edom will be punished for its hostility to Judah. The children of Israel will reoccupy their land.

✦ **HAGGAI**

Written to encourage the rebuilding of the Temple. Now the Temple foundations have been laid, the people will be blessed.

✦ **ZECHARIAH**

Contains a call to repentance and a series of visions relating to the restoration of Jerusalem; the last six chapters may have been written later and have a strong messianic tone.

✦ **MALACHI**

Calls for a renewal in worship and renewed faithfulness to the Covenant. If the people repent, the nation will prosper. Before the 'great and dreadful' day of the Lord comes, God will send Elijah.

JONAH, THE RELUCTANT PROPHET

Jonah was an 8th-century BC prophet mentioned in 2 Kings 14, but the book named after him seems to be of a later date.

JONAH RUNS AWAY FROM GOD

Commanded by God to preach repentance to the Assyrian city of Nineveh because of its great wickedness, Jonah immediately heads off in the opposite direction, boarding a ship for faraway Tarshish (which probably means Spain). God causes a severe storm to arise, and Jonah and the terrified sailors draw lots to determine who it is that has so displeased some god or other. The lot falls on Jonah.

> 'Jonah' has become proverbial for someone who brings bad luck.

THE WHALE

At Jonah's own suggestion, the sailors throw him overboard, and the storm subsides. God sends a large fish to swallow Jonah, and he remains in the fish's stomach for three days and nights, praying to God. At God's command, the fish then spits him out onto dry land.

The Book of Jonah doesn't actually talk about a whale. Jonah is swallowed by a 'great fish'. The reference to a whale comes in the words of Jesus in Matthew 12:40.

NINEVEH

Once more, God commands Jonah to go to Nineveh, and this time Jonah obeys. Once in the city, Jonah proclaims God's warning. The people of Nineveh heed Jonah's proclamation and repent; everyone, even the king himself, puts on sackcloth, fasts and prays to God, and they give up their wickedness. Seeing that the people of Nineveh have repented and reformed, God decides not to destroy the city after all.

Sackcloth was a coarse black cloth, usually made from goats' hair. It was customarily worn as a sign of mourning or repentance.

The gourd plant

Rather than being pleased that his mission has brought about the reform of the Ninevites and that God will not now be destroying the city, Jonah is furious. He complains to God that he always knew that this is what would happen, because God is a gracious and merciful god. Jonah storms out of the city and sits down, apparently still hoping that something might happen to Nineveh. God makes a tall shady plant grow up to give Jonah shelter. The next day it is destroyed by a worm. When Jonah again complains, God points out that if Jonah is concerned about the destruction of the plant, which he did nothing to create, is it not right that God would want to avoid the destruction of Nineveh.

THE MESSAGE OF THE BOOK

What message is the story of Jonah intended to convey? There is certainly a message that God is gracious and merciful, 'slow to anger and of great kindness'. And since Nineveh, capital of Assyria, the enemy of Israel, is spared by God, the book also teaches that God's mercy extends even to the enemies of the Jews.

Jesus refers to the story of Jonah (Matthew 12:39–41) and draws a parallel between Jonah's three days and nights in the stomach of the fish and the three days and nights that he will pass 'in the heart of the earth' between his death and resurrection. In fact, Jesus spends two nights in the grave.

DANIEL, A FAITHFUL JEW IN A FOREIGN LAND

Daniel is one of the gifted young men of the leading families of Judah taken to Babylon at the orders of the king, Nebuchadnezzar, to be trained in the Babylonian language and learning. While some scholars believe that the book was written in the 6th century BC, others believe that it was in fact written during the 2nd century BC to encourage the Jewish people to keep the faith at a time when they were suffering religious oppression. Whatever the truth, Daniel has been accepted as a prophet by Jews and Christians, and Jesus himself refers to Daniel as a prophet (Matthew 24:15).

FACTFILE

Name: DANIEL (BABYLONIAN NAME: BELTESHAZZAR)
Companions: HANANIAH (SHADRACH), MISHAEL (MESHACH), AZARIAH (ABED-NEGO)

STORIES ABOUT DANIEL AND HIS COMPANIONS

DANIEL'S REFUSAL TO EAT BABYLONIAN FOOD

Daniel and his three companions refuse to eat Babylonian food that would not have been prepared in accordance with the dietary rules of the Mosaic Law. For ten days they eat only vegetables and drink only water, and at the end of this time they look healthier than others who have been eating the Babylonian food. They are therefore allowed to continue eating their own food.

✦

NEBUCHADNEZZAR'S FIRST DREAM

God gives Daniel 'understanding in all visions and dreams' (1:17). King Nebuchadnezzar has a dream, the content and meaning of which God

reveals to Daniel in a vision. Daniel then describes and interprets the dream to Nebuchadnezzar. In his dream, the king

has seen a statue of gold, silver, bronze, iron and clay shattered by a rock that falls on it. Daniel tells Nebuchadnezzar that he (the king) is the gold, and that the silver, bronze and iron represent empires that will follow the Babylonians, the mixture of iron and clay showing that the last empire will be divided. This empire will be followed by a kingdom established by God, a kingdom that will last forever. For his ability at interpreting dreams, Daniel is promoted to be head of all the wise men in Babylon.

✦

THE FIERY FURNACE

Nebuchadnezzar sets up a gold statue and commands everyone in the empire to worship it. Shadrach, Meshach and Abed-nego refuse to do so, and for this disobedience are thrown into a furnace. But the king and his officials see four figures in the furnace: God has sent an angel to rescue the young men, who walk out of the furnace unharmed.

✦

NEBUCHADNEZZAR'S SECOND DREAM

In a second dream, Nebuchadnezzar sees a tree growing up to heaven, loaded with fruit and giving shade and shelter to birds and animals. But an angel appears and orders it cut down, leaving only a stump. Daniel explains to Nebuchadnezzar that he, a strong and powerful king, is the tree. Just as the tree was cut down, so he will lose his kingdom, but just as a stump remained,

so will the kingdom be restored to him. The angel has also prophesied that during this time the king will lose his mind and live like an animal for seven years. All this comes to pass a year later.

✦

BELSHAZZAR'S FEAST

The story now passes to the next king, Belshazzar. During a banquet, a hand is seen writing on the wall the words *MENE, MENE, TEKEL, UPHARSIN.* Daniel explains to the king that *MENE* means 'numbered', *TEKEL* means 'weighed' and *PARSIN* means 'divided':

God has numbered the days of Belshazzar's reign and is bringing it to an end; Belshazzar has been weighed on scales and found wanting; and his kingdom is to be divided up and given to the Medes and Persians.

The four words are Aramaic, not Hebrew. 'U' means 'and'; the fourth word means 'and PARSIN'. There is a play on words in this prophecy, in that the Aramaic word for 'divided' sounds like the word for 'Persians'.

'In that night was Belshazzar the king of the Chaldeans slain. And Darius the Median took the kingdom' (5:30–31).

THE KING WAS PROBABLY CYRUS, NOT DARIUS (SEE PAGE 139).

DANIEL IN THE LIONS' DEN

Darius appoints Daniel as a senior official in his kingdom. Jealous, the other officials try to find a way of bringing Daniel down. They persuade the king to issue a decree that for 30 days no one is to ask for anything from any god or from any person except the king. Daniel, however, continues to pray to God, not in secret but quite openly. He is denounced to the king, who is forced against his will by his own law – the 'law of the Medes and Persians, which altereth not' – to condemn Daniel to death in a lion pit. After a sleepless night, the king, fearing the worst, opens up the pit, and is delighted to find Daniel alive and well: God has sent an angel to keep the lions' mouths closed.

Daniel's visions

The second part of the Book of Daniel describes four visions that Daniel had during the reigns of Belshazzar, Darius and Cyrus. These have been the subject of a great deal of analysis and speculation among Jews and Christians, particularly regarding the times and events mentioned.

STORIES IN THE APOCRYPHA ABOUT DANIEL AND HIS COMPANIONS

The History of Susanna

Susanna is a beautiful and pious young Jewish woman living in Babylon. Two old men, judges in the Jewish community, fall in love with her. Hoping to find her alone, they one day hide in her garden. When Susanna comes out into the garden to bathe, the elders try to persuade her to have sex with them. When she refuses, they pretend that they have found her having sex with a young man who ran away when the elders spied them. The next day Susanna is put on trial, and because of the elders' testimony against her, is condemned to death for adultery. Susanna prays to God, and God moves Daniel to speak up for her. He accuses the elders of lying, and proves it by interrogating them separately and showing an inconsistency in their stories: one claims that Susanna and the young man were together under a mastic tree, the other says it was a holm tree. Susanna is vindicated, and the elders are condemned to the death they sought for her.

A Daniel come to judgement

The name Daniel became proverbial for someone who is wise beyond his years. In The *Merchant of Venice*, Shakespeare has Shylock say, when speaking of Portia, who he believes is supporting his case in a lawsuit:

> *A Daniel come to judgment! yea, a Daniel!*
> *O wise young judge, how I do honour thee!*

THE SONG OF THE THREE HOLY CHILDREN

The Song of the Three Holy Children is set at the point in the Book of Daniel where Hananiah, Mishael and Azariah (Shadrach, Meshach and Abed-nego) have been thrown into the furnace for disobeying the decree of Nebuchadnezzar. This short book consists of a prayer said by Azariah when they are thrown into the furnace, and a further prayer of praise and thanksgiving said by all three when the angel rescues them from the flames.

BEL AND THE DRAGON

In Bel and the Dragon, Daniel is challenged by the Babylonian king to prove that the idol of the god Bel is not a living god and does not consume the food offered to it each day. By secretly scattering ashes on the floor of the temple, Daniel shows that it was the priests and their families who secretly entered the temple by night and ate the food offerings and drank the wine offerings, because they have left footprints in the ashes. The priests are executed and Daniel is allowed to destroy the idol of Bel and its temple. The Babylonians also worship a dragon, and since this is not an idol but a living creature, the king orders Daniel to worship it. Daniel says he will only worship the Lord, and asks the king's permission to kill the dragon if he can. The king agrees. Daniel feeds the dragon lumps of a mixture of tar, fat and hair, and the dragon bursts. However, the Babylonians are enraged, and Daniel is once again thrown into the lions' den, this time for six days. He of course survives (although the lions are deliberately starved to make them particularly hungry), and is released by the king on the seventh day.

THE OTHER BOOKS OF THE APOCRYPHA

1 Esdras	Esdras is the Ezra of the Old Testament. 1 Esdras is essentially another version of the Book of Ezra, with some of Nehemiah and some additional material.
2 Esdras	Chapters 3 to 14 of this book comprise seven visions supposedly seen by Ezra. Like Job, Ezra cannot understand why the righteous suffer. The book looks to a future new Jerusalem.
Tobit	Tobit's son collects some money, overcomes a demon, gets himself a wife, and cures his father's blindness, all with the aid of an angel.
Judith	Judith is a Jewish woman who kills the Assyrian general Holofernes when the Assyrians are besieging the town of Bethulia where she lives.
Additions to Esther	Short passages which expand on some sections of the Book of Esther.
The Wisdom of Solomon	Not written by King Solomon; in part of the book, Wisdom is personified as a lady; false worship is condemned and God's justice is vindicated
Ecclesiasticus	Also called the Wisdom of Jesus the son of Sirach; a book of wise advice similar to Proverbs.
Baruch	Comprises a prayer of Baruch, a reproach to Israel for having abandoned the Law, a poem about wisdom, a promise of restoration, and a letter supposedly written by Jeremiah.
The Prayer of Manasseh	Supposedly a prayer of King Manasseh when he was captive in Babylon (2 Chronicles 33:13).
1 & 2 Maccabees	Two books which both tell of the attempted suppression of Judaism by Antiochus IV and of the Jewish revolt led by Judas Maccabaeus.

NEW TESTAMENT TIMELINE

The dates in this timeline cannot be exact: authorities vary in their dating of most of these events.

c. 7–5BC	BIRTH OF JESUS
4BC	DEATH OF HEROD THE GREAT
c. 26–29	BAPTISM OF JESUS
c. 30–33	THE CRUCIFIXION
c.34–35	SAUL'S CONVERSION
c. 46–48	PAUL'S FIRST MISSIONARY JOURNEY
c. 49–50	JERUSALEM COUNCIL OF THE CHURCH (ACTS 15)
c. 50–52	PAUL'S SECOND MISSIONARY JOURNEY
c. 53–57	PAUL'S THIRD MISSIONARY JOURNEY
c. 57–61	PAUL'S IMPRISONMENT IN CAESAREA
c. 60–67	PAUL'S TWO PERIODS OF IMPRISONMENT IN ROME
c. 64–67	PETER'S EXECUTION IN ROME
c. 64–67	PAUL'S EXECUTION IN ROME

Four Roman emperors are mentioned in the New Testament:
Augustus (63BC–AD14) ❖ *Tiberius (47BC–AD37)* ❖ *Claudius (10BC–AD54)* ❖
Nero (AD37–68)

THE GOSPELS: THE STORY OF JESUS

THE GOSPEL WRITERS

✳ It is not certain who wrote Matthew's gospel. The linking of this gospel to the apostle Matthew is a late tradition.

✳ According to tradition, Mark's gospel was written in Rome by a Mark who was Peter's translator (perhaps Peter's Greek wasn't very good!). He may have been the John Mark of Acts 12 and 15.

✳ Luke's gospel and Acts were written by a person who seems to have been present during some of the episodes described in Acts, where the writer speaks of 'we' (e.g. 16:10–17).

✳ John's gospel is traditionally ascribed to the apostle John.

✳ Ancient Christian symbols for the four evangelists were:

MATTHEW – *a man* ✳ MARK – *a lion* ✳ LUKE – *an ox* ✳ JOHN – *an eagle*

These symbols are taken from Revelation 4:7. All usually have wings.

✳ Matthew's, Mark's and Luke's gospels are known as the 'Synoptic Gospels' (from Greek *syn* together + *opsis* a view) because they are written from the same point of view. John's gospel is written from a different perspective.

✳ The gospels were not the first New Testament books to be written. Paul's letters are earlier.

✳ Theologians have given the name 'Q' (from German *Quelle*, meaning 'source') to a source of material apparently used by Matthew and Luke when they wrote their gospels. Q consisted almost entirely of sayings of Jesus.

The birth of Jesus

In the beginning was the Word, and the Word was with God, and the Word was God. And the Word was made flesh, and dwelt among us. (John 1:1, 14)

The Annunciation

God sends the angel Gabriel to a virgin, Mary. Gabriel greets Mary:

'Hail, thou that art highly favoured, the Lord is with thee: Blessed art thou among women. Behold, thou shalt conceive in thy womb, and bring forth a son, and shalt call his name JESUS. He shall be great, and shall be called the Son of the Highest: and the Lord God shall give unto him the throne of his father David: And he shall reign over the house of Jacob for ever; and of his kingdom there shall be no end.' (Luke 1:26–33)

The angel's salutation to Mary forms the basis of a well-known prayer known as the Hail Mary or, in Latin, Ave Maria.

THE VIRGIN BIRTH

When Joseph finds that Mary is expecting a baby which is not his, he is not sure he should marry her. The angel of the Lord appears to him in a dream, saying:

'Joseph, thou son of David, fear not to take unto thee Mary thy wife: for that which is conceived in her is of the Holy Ghost. And she shall bring forth a son, and thou shalt call his name JESUS: for he shall save his people from their sins.'
(Matthew 1:18–21)

'Jesus' comes from the Aramaic form of the Hebrew name 'Joshua'. It means 'God saves'.

The Virgin Birth refers to Jesus' birth. The Immaculate Conception is a doctrine of the Roman Catholic Church that Mary was born without the stain of original sin.

The fulfilment of prophecy

Now all this was done, that it might be fulfilled which was spoken of the Lord by the prophet, saying, Behold, a virgin shall be with child, and shall bring forth a son, and they shall call his name Emmanuel, which being interpreted is, God with us. (Matthew 1:22–23; the prophecy is that of Isaiah 7:14)

THE BIRTH OF JESUS

The birth of Jesus is described in only two of the four gospels: Matthew and Luke. Matthew mentions the wise men, Luke mentions the shepherds.

IN THE BLEAK MID-WINTER

In the bleak mid-winter
A stable-place sufficed
The Lord God Almighty,
Jesus Christ.

Christina Rossetti

The Bible doesn't tell us when Jesus was born. We know neither the year nor the time of the year of his birth.

ANNO DOMINI

Jesus must have been born before the death of Herod the Great in 4BC. This means that our counting of dates BC (= 'before Christ') and AD (= *Anno Domini* 'in the year of our Lord') is not strictly accurate.

CHRISTMAS

This is celebrated on 25 December by western churches, but on 7 January by most Orthodox churches. The earliest mention of Christmas being celebrated on 25 December dates from the middle of the 4th century.

THE STABLE

There is no mention of a stable in the Bible. Luke's gospel says that there was no room in the inn and that Mary laid Jesus in a manger, which has given rise to the assumption that they must have been in a stable. The Church of the Nativity in Bethlehem is in fact built over a cave or grotto that tradition has it was the birthplace of Jesus, and a cave is referred to by some early Christian writers. There is also no mention by Luke of any animals in the stable: the ox and ass of Christmas carols are taken from Isaiah 1:3: 'The ox knoweth his owner, and the ass his master's crib'.

THE SHEPHERDS

According to the 13th-century *Book of the Bee*, there were seven shepherds and their names were Asher, Barshabba, Jose, Joseph, Justus, Nicodemus and Zebulan.

THE WISE MEN FROM THE EAST

Nothing is known for certain about the wise men who came from the east to find Jesus, but there are many stories and traditions:

✳ The Bible does not say that there were three wise men; this assumption is based on the fact that they brought three gifts: gold, frankincense and myrrh. In some traditions, there are twelve wise men who travel to Bethlehem.

✳ The Bible does not give their names, but later tradition generally names them Melchior, Gaspar (or Caspar) and Balthazar. (A different tradition gives them the names Hor, Basanater and Karsudan.)

✳ Melchior is said to mean 'king of light', Gaspar 'the white one' and Balthazar 'lord of treasures'.

✳ The Bible does not say that they were kings, but later traditions identify them as kings of Persia, India and Arabia, or of India, Chaldea and Persia, or from Asia, Africa and Europe.

✳ One tradition makes them descendants respectively of Shem, Ham and Japheth, Noah's three sons.

✳ The Bible does not say that the wise men visited Jesus in the stable. In fact, since King Herod kills all the boy babies around Bethlehem up to the age of two (Matthew 1:16), it seems clear that the visit of the wise men took place some time after the birth of Jesus.

✳ The Bible does not say what sort of 'wise men' these travellers were. 'Magi' belonged to a Persian religious group dedicated to astrology, divination and interpreting dreams, which would explain their interest in the new star they had seen.

✳ The Bible does not say that each wise

man presented one gift, but according to later tradition, Melchior offered the gold, Gaspar the frankincense and Balthazar the myrrh.

✳ It has been suggested that gold was given in recognition of Jesus as king, the frankincense in recognition of his right to our worship, and the myrrh as a prophetic recognition of the suffering and death he would go through. Myrrh was used as a painkiller and in embalming the dead.

✳ The medieval traveller Marco Polo writes of a different tradition among the Zoroastrians in Persia, according to which the magi set out to seek the child, carrying gold, frankincense and myrrh, not as gifts but as a way of ascertaining the nature of the child: if he took the gold, he was a king; if the incense, he was God; and if the myrrh, a healer. Jesus accepted all three gifts – king, God and healer.

✳ There is a shrine in Cologne Cathedral believed to hold relics of the three kings.

JESUS: FROM BABY TO BAPTISM

The Bible says little about Jesus' life between his birth and his baptism:

✟ *Following the Jewish Law (Leviticus 12), Jesus is circumcised on the eighth day after his birth, and about a month later Mary and Joseph go to the Temple in Jerusalem for the ceremony of purification (Luke 2:21–23); at the Temple, Jesus is recognized as the Messiah by Simeon.*

✟ *Fearing Herod, Joseph takes his family to Egypt (Matthew 2); when he returns, he sets up home again in Nazareth.*

✟ *Jesus 'grew, and waxed strong in spirit, filled with wisdom: and the grace of God was upon him'. (Luke 2:40)*

✟ *When Jesus is 12 years old, he accompanies his parents to Jerusalem for the Passover. On their journey home, Mary and Joseph discover that Jesus is not travelling with their party. Returning to Jerusalem, they find him at the Temple, discussing religion with the Jewish teachers. 'And all that heard him were astonished at his understanding and answers.' (Luke 2:47)*

JESUS' BROTHERS were *James, Joses, Simon* and *Judas* (Matthew 13:55). Jesus also had sisters (13:55). Some Christians believe these were children of Joseph, but not of Mary. James became a leader of the church in Jerusalem, and was martyred.

Jesus in England

And did those feet in ancient time
Walk upon England's mountains green?
And was the Holy Lamb of God
On England's pleasant pastures seen?
William Blake

There is an old tradition that Jesus came to England as a boy with Joseph of Arimathea, said to have been Mary's uncle and a merchant with tin-mining interests around Glastonbury in south-west England.

Jesus' baptism and temptation

When Jesus is baptized by John, he sees heaven open and the Holy Spirit coming down in the form of a dove. A voice is heard: 'This is my beloved son, in whom I am well pleased.' (Matthew 3:17) Jesus then spends 40 days in the wilderness, where he successfully rejects Satan's temptations.

THE TWELVE APOSTLES

Jesus calls together all his disciples, and from them chooses twelve 'whom also he named apostles' (Luke 6:13). These twelve men are commissioned by Jesus to go to 'the lost sheep of the house of Israel' to preach that the kingdom of heaven was near at hand, and to heal the sick, cleanse lepers, raise the dead and cast out devils (Matthew 10:7–8). These twelve apostles, although chosen from among a larger group of disciples, are also referred to as the 'twelve disciples' (e.g. Matthew 10:1 and 11:1).

The Greek word *apostolos* means 'someone who is sent', and implies being chosen for a special purpose. It is used more than 80 times in the New Testament.

The twelve apostles			
MATTHEW 10:2–4	MARK 3:16–19	LUKE 6:14–16	ACTS 1:13
Simon, called Peter	Simon	Simon	Peter
Andrew	Andrew	Andrew	Andrew
James	James	James	James
John	John	John	John
Philip	Philip	Philip	Philip
Bartholomew	Bartholomew	Bartholomew	Bartholomew
Thomas	Thomas	Thomas	Thomas
Matthew	Matthew	Matthew	Matthew
James (son of Alphaeus)	James (son of Alphaeus)	James (son of Alphaeus)	James (son of Alphaeus)
Lebbaeus (surnamed Thaddaeus)	Thaddaeus		
Simon the Canaanite	Simon the Canaanite	Simon called Zelotes	Simon Zelotes
		Judas (brother of James)	Judas (brother of James)
Judas Iscariot	Judas Iscariot	Judas Iscariot	

Significance of the number '12'

The importance of Jesus' choosing twelve apostles is perhaps shown in Matthew 19:28, where he promises Peter that the apostles will 'sit upon twelve thrones, judging the twelve tribes of Israel'. After the death of Judas Iscariot, the disciples chose Matthias to fill the twelfth place (Acts 1:26).

The Seventy

Luke 10:1 tells us that Jesus commissioned a further 70 people (or 72, according to some manuscripts of the Bible), who were sent out with a similar remit to that of the original twelve. Of these 70 nothing more is known, except that their mission was successful (Luke 10:17).

OTHER APOSTLES

Other people are called 'apostle' in the New Testament. One of these is, of course, Paul, who says that he was 'called to be an apostle' (Romans 1:1), and refers to himself as an apostle of Jesus Christ at the beginning of most of his letters. Paul saw himself specifically as the apostle to the Gentiles (Romans 11:13). Paul also speaks of Jesus' brother James as an apostle (Galatians 1:19). In Acts 14:4, Paul and Barnabas are referred to as apostles, and at the end of his letter to the Romans, Paul mentions his relatives Andronicus and Junia (or Junias) who are 'of note among the apostles'.

APOSTLES' CREED

The Apostles' Creed is one of the ancient creeds of the Christian faith. The early church believed, incorrectly, that it had been written by the Twelve Apostles.

Apostle spoons

Apostle spoons are silver spoons with figures on their handles representing the Twelve Apostles. Found as single spoons or in sets of twelve (also sets of thirteen, one larger spoon having the figure of Christ on it), they were once commonly given as christening presents.

PETER

FACTFILE	
Name: SIMEON (HEBREW) OR SIMON (GREEK)	*Brother:* ANDREW
Nickname: PETER (OR CEPHAS; ARAMAIC KEPHA) 'THE ROCK'	*Home town:* BETHSAIDA IN GALILEE
	Occupation: FISHERMAN
Father: JONAH	*Marital status:* MARRIED (HIS MOTHER-IN-LAW IS HEALED BY JESUS, MARK 1:30)

Peter's call to be a disciple of Jesus comes one day when Jesus sees Peter and Andrew fishing by the Sea of Galilee. Jesus says to them: 'Follow me, and I will make you fishers of men'. And straight away they leave their nets to follow him. (Matthew 4:18–20)

John's gospel has a slightly different account. There we are told that it was Andrew who first found Jesus and told Peter about him (John 1:42). This could, of course, have happened at some time before the call described in Matthew's gospel.

Peter is one of what appears to be an 'inner circle' of three disciples – Peter, James and John. It is these three that Jesus takes with him when he goes to heal Jairus' daughter (Mark 5:37–42), it is these three who witness the Transfiguration (Matthew 17), and it is again these three who are with Jesus in Gethsemane (Matthew 26:37).

THREE INCIDENTS THAT SHOW PETER'S CHARACTER

PETER TRIES TO WALK ON WATER
(MATTHEW 14:29–30)

During a storm, when the disciples are in a boat on the Sea of Galilee, they see Jesus walking towards them across the water. Peter jumps out of the ship to walk to him, but in the stormy wind he loses his nerve and begins to sink. He cries out to Jesus: Lord, save me. And Jesus catches hold of him, chiding him for his loss of faith.

✽

PETER IS UNWILLING TO LET JESUS WASH HIS FEET (JOHN 13:5–9)

Peter is unwilling to let Jesus wash his feet, but when Jesus tells him that he cannot be a disciple unless he allows this, Peter immediately jumps to the other extreme and asks his Master to wash not only his feet, but his hands and his head as well!

✳

PETER DENIES JESUS (LUKE 22:33–34 & 54–62)

At the Last Supper, Peter promises Jesus that he is ready to go to prison with him, even to die with him if need be. Jesus replies that in fact Peter will deny him three times before the cock crows for morning. Later, after Jesus has been arrested and taken to the High Priest's house, Peter again loses his nerve and three times denies knowing Jesus.

Weathercocks

It is said that a 9th-century pope decreed that the figure of a cock should be set up on every church steeple as an emblem of St Peter and in allusion to this incident. Opinions differ as to whether the weathercock story is fact or fable.

PETRELS

Petrels are small seabirds. They take their name from Peter because of his attempt to walk to Jesus across the water of the Sea of Galilee. Storm petrels fly low over the sea with their legs dangling and patting the surface, so appearing to walk on the water.

PETER THE ROCK

Despite Peter's impetuosity, his sometimes wavering faith, and his ability to say the wrong thing (Matthew 16:22), Jesus sees the true character of the man. Peter is the rock on which Jesus will build his church (Matthew 16:18); it is Peter who will strengthen the other disciples (Luke 22:32); and it is to Peter that Jesus entrusts the 'feeding of his lambs and sheep' (John 21:15–17). Peter, James and John are named by Paul as pillars of the church (Galatians 2:9).

It is perhaps significant that, after Peter's denial of Jesus three times before the Crucifixion, when Jesus entrusts the church to Peter's care after the Resurrection (John 21), he leads Peter to affirm his love three times.

PETER IN THE EARLY CHURCH

By the beginning of the Acts of the Apostles, Peter is clearly the leader of the disciples. It is he who preaches the first two Christian sermons, to the disciples in Acts 1 and to the people of Jerusalem in Acts 2. A key incident for the development of the church is God's revelation to Peter in a vision of ritually unclean birds and animals (Acts 10) that the new covenant is not just for Jews but also for Gentiles, and that Jews and Gentile Christians can come together as equals; Peter then baptizes the Roman centurion Cornelius and his family. Peter later speaks out against requiring non-Jewish converts to be circumcised and to obey the Mosaic Law (Acts 15:7–11), though in the face of opposition from traditionalist Jewish Christians he appears to have wavered at one point (Galatians 2:11–14), for which he is criticized by Paul.

PETER IN ROME

Tradition has it that Peter was the first bishop of Rome. He was martyred during a period of persecution of Christians by the emperor Nero between AD64 and 68. According to the apocryphal Acts of Peter, he was, at his own request, crucified head downwards, and tradition has it that he was buried at a spot now below the altar of the Vatican basilica.

✤ FEAST DAY: *29 June*

As Peter was a fisherman, several species of fish have been given the name 'St Peter's fish'. Among these are the tilapia (found in the Sea of Galilee), and the haddock and the dory (both said to bear the marks of Peter's fingers). 'Peterman' is an old word for a fisherman.

THE OTHER DISCIPLES

ANDREW

We know much less about Peter's brother Andrew than we do about Peter. After being listed among the disciples in Acts 1, he is never mentioned again in the New Testament. Like 'Peter', 'Andrew' is a Greek name, meaning 'manly'. If Andrew had a Hebrew name, there is no record of it. According to tradition, he evangelized in what is now Turkey and Greece, and was crucified on an X-shaped cross at Patras, in Greece.

✤ FEAST DAY: *30 November*

JAMES AND JOHN

FACTFILE	
Relationship: BROTHERS	rather quick-tempered)
Parents: ZEBEDEE AND SALOME	*James* IS OFTEN CALLED 'JAMES THE
Occupation: FISHERMEN	GREAT/GREATER' TO DISTINGUISH HIM
Nickname: BOANERGES (= 'sons of	FROM THE OTHER APOSTLE JAMES, WHO IS
thunder', apparently from their being	'JAMES THE LESS'

- James and John are the next disciples to be called by Jesus after Peter and Andrew (Matthew 4:21). Peter, James and John seem to form an inner circle among the disciples, accompanying Jesus on special occasions (see page 162), but they also upset the other disciples by asking to be given privileged places beside the throne of Jesus (Mark 10:37; in Matthew 20:21, it is their mother who makes this request).
- James was the first of the apostles to be martyred, executed by King Herod Agrippa I (Acts 12:1–2). There is a tradition that he had preached the gospel in Spain, and that his body was taken to Spain after his death. His shrine at Compostela was a great medieval centre of pilgrimage.
- Tradition identifies John as 'the disciple whom Jesus loved' (John 13:23, 19:26). He was the only apostle to witness the Crucifixion from close by. One gospel and three letters are attributed to him, but there are linguistic grounds for crediting Revelation to a different writer. He probably died at Ephesus (now in Turkey) c. 100.

✤ FEAST DAY OF ST JOHN: *western churches 27 December, eastern churches 6 May*

✤ FEAST DAY OF ST JAMES: *25 July*

MATTHEW

Matthew was the fifth of the apostles Jesus called. It is generally accepted that Matthew the tax collector (Matthew 9:9) is the same person as Levi the tax collector (Mark 2:14, Luke 5:27). 'Matthew' means 'gift of Yahweh'. The first gospel is attributed to him, though many scholars doubt that he wrote it as it stands, and after being mentioned in the list of apostles in Acts 1, nothing else is known for certain about him. Although both Levi and James are said to be sons of Alphaeus, there is no evidence that they were related: they are never referred to as brothers. There are unreliable traditions that he was an evangelist in Ethiopia (to the south of the Caspian Sea), Persia and other places. The manner of his death is not certain, but he was probably martyred.

In the Middle Ages, Matthew is sometimes depicted with glasses (which weren't invented till around the 13th century), presumably to help him read his account books!

✤ FEAST DAY: *western churches 21 September, eastern churches 16 November*

THOMAS

Thomas is also called Didymus (e.g. John 11:16). Both names, the first Aramaic, the second Greek, mean 'twin', but nothing is known of a twin brother or sister. He is named in all four gospels and in Acts, but we learn most about him in John's gospel.

He is a man of courage, willing to die with Jesus (11:16), but also a cautious man, unwilling to believe in the resurrection until he sees Jesus for himself (20:24–29), but on being convinced, declares Jesus to be his Lord and his God. Of his activities in the early church nothing is known for certain, but there is a tradition that he took the gospel to southern India in AD52, where he established several churches to which the present-day Mar Thoma (St Thomas) Christians trace their origins. According to some traditions, he was murdered, by one or more Hindus, at Chennai.

✤ FEAST DAY: *21 December*

BARTHOLOMEW/NATHANAEL

About the five remaining disciples (not counting Judas), little is said in the Bible, and even less is known about their later careers, though all have traditions attached to their names. It is generally accepted that Bartholomew (= 'son of Tolmai') and Nathanael are the same person. He came from Cana, and was introduced to Jesus by Philip. Jesus calls him 'an Israelite in whom is no guile' (John 1:47). Later traditions have him preaching in any of various places such as Egypt, Persia, and near the Black Sea. He is said to have been flayed alive and beheaded.

FEAST DAY: *24 August*

PHILIP

Philip came from Bethsaida, and introduced Nathanael to Jesus. He is not the same person as Philip the evangelist (Acts 21:8), who was one of the deacons appointed by the early church (Acts 6:5), but later church traditions confused them. It is the deacon Philip who preached in Samaria and explained the gospel to the Ethiopian eunuch (Acts 8). Nothing further is known about the apostle. One or other Philip, or both, may have died at Hierapolis, in what is now Turkey.

FEAST DAY: *western churches 3 May, eastern churches 14 November.*

JAMES, SON OF ALPHAEUS

Also known as 'James the Less', probably because he was either shorter or younger than John's brother James. He may have been the brother or father of Judas (= Thaddaeus). Some equate him with James 'the Lord's brother', who was a leader of the Christians in Jerusalem. Nothing further is known about him; a late tradition speaks of his martyrdom in Persia.

FEAST DAY: *western churches 1 May; eastern churches 9 October*

JUDAS/THADDAEUS/LEBBAEUS

It is generally accepted that Thaddaeus, Lebbaeus and Judas the brother (or son) of James are the same person, though the 4th-century writer Eusebius names Thaddaeus as one of the Seventy, not one of the Twelve (see page 161). Nothing is known about his activities in the early church, although some identify him as the writer of the Letter of Jude. He may have been martyred in Persia along with Simon. As a saint, he is generally known as St Jude.

FEAST DAY: *western churches 28 October, eastern churches 19 June.*

SIMON THE ZEALOT

In the Authorized Version of the Bible, Simon is twice called 'Simon the Canaanite' (Matthew 10:4, Mark 3:18). This is not intended to mean he was an inhabitant of Canaan but rather that he was a Cananean or Zealot, a member of a militant Jewish group strongly opposed to Roman rule in Palestine. Nothing more is known about him; a later tradition has him preaching in Egypt and Persia, and being martyred in Persia, perhaps along with St Jude.

FEAST DAY: *28 October*

MATTHIAS

Matthias was chosen as the replacement for Judas Iscariot (Acts 1:21–26). He is never mentioned again in the Bible. Nothing is known about him, though according to various traditions, he preached to the Jews and in the area near the Black Sea. He may have been crucified or stoned to death.

FEAST DAY: *western churches 14 May, eastern churches 9 August*

JUDAS ISCARIOT – THE APOSTLE
WHO BETRAYED JESUS

Judas is the only apostle who was not from Galilee. 'Iscariot' means 'from Kerioth', and Kerioth was a village in southern Judea. According to John (13:18), Jesus chose Judas to be an apostle knowing that he would betray him, quoting from Psalm 41:9:

'He that eateth bread with me hath lifted up his heel against me.'

JUDAS TREE

The elder tree is known as the Judas tree, from a tradition that Judas hanged himself on one. Another tree, Cercis siliquastrum, *has the same name for the same reason.*

Judas and money

Judas was the group treasurer, in charge of 'the bag' (John 12:6, 13:29). While in Matthew (26:8–9) and Mark (14:4) several people complain that pouring perfume over Jesus' head is a waste of money that could have been given to the poor, in John's gospel it is specifically Judas who complains – not, John says, because he cared about the poor but because he was a thief (12:6). This establishes money as a possible motive for Judas' betrayal of Jesus – the 30 pieces of silver he is promised by the chief priests (Matthew 26:15), an implicit allusion to Zechariah 11:12.

JUDAS' DEATH

According to Matthew 27, Judas repents of what he has done and takes the money back to the priests. When they refuse it, he throws it down and goes off and hangs himself. The priests use the money to buy a field for a cemetery for foreigners. In Acts 1, it is said that Judas bought the field himself, whereupon he fell down, burst open and died.

Why did Judas do it?

Was it for the money? Was it Satan (Luke 22:3)? Was it disappointment in Jesus? Was it to force Jesus to openly declare himself the Messiah? Who knows?

SYMBOLS OF THE TWELVE APOSTLES

Each of the Apostles is associated with an emblem, usually depicting some aspect of his life or death. Lists of these emblems vary, and some apostles are associated with more than one symbol.

PETER ❶ *two crossed keys or a bunch of keys, because Jesus said he would give Peter 'the keys of the kingdom of heaven' (Matthew 16:19)* ❷ *a cock, because after denying Jesus three times, Peter wept when he heard the cock crow (Matthew 26:74–75)* ❸ *a chain, because he was chained in prison (Acts 12)* ❹ *an upside-down cross, because tradition has it that is how he was martyred*

ANDREW ❶ *an X-shaped cross, because according to a tradition dating from the Middle Ages, he was crucified on a cross of that shape* ❷ *a fishing net, because he was a fisherman*

JAMES THE GREATER *a pilgrim's staff, a scallop-shell or a bottle, because he is the patron saint of pilgrims (a scallop-shell was the pilgrim's badge in the Middle Ages)*

JOHN ❶ *a cup with a winged serpent or dragon flying out of it, from the tradition that when challenged to drink a cup of poison, John made the sign of a cross over it, and Satan like a dragon flew from it, and the poison was gone* ❷ *an eagle (as an evangelist – see page 154)*

PHILIP ❶ *a long staff surmounted with a cross, because tradition says he was martyred by being suspended by the neck from a tall pillar* ❷ *loaves of bread because of his doubts about where to find bread to feed the 5000 (John 6)*

BARTHOLOMEW *a knife, because he was martyred by being flayed and then beheaded*

THOMAS ❶ *a spear, because he was killed with a spear* ❷ *a T-square; one tradition has it that he built a palace for an Indian king*

MATTHEW ❶ *a spear, sword or halberd, from traditions about how he was martyred* ❷ *a money bag or box, because he was a tax collector* ❸ *a winged man (see page 154)*

JAMES THE LESS *a fuller's pole, because he was killed by a blow to the head with a pole by Simeon the fuller*

SIMON (THE ZEALOT) ❶ *a saw, because according to one tradition he was sawn to death* ❷ *a curved sword, again from the supposed manner of his death*

JUDAS (BROTHER OF JAMES) ❶ *a club, because tradition has it he was martyred with a club* ❷ *Simon and Judas are sometimes depicted together, Simon holding a fish and Judas a boat, from the belief that they too were fishermen*

JUDAS ISCARIOT ❶ *a bag, because he 'had the bag and bare what was put therein' (John 12:6)* ❷ *a noose, because he hanged himself.*

THE HORRID HERODS

The name Herod occurs more than 20 times in the New Testament. Jesus was born 'in the days of Herod the king'; it was 'Herod the tetrarch' who beheaded John the Baptist; another 'Herod the king' executed the apostle James. So who were all these Herods?

HEROD THE GREAT

Herod the Great is the Herod who was king at the time of Jesus' birth (Matthew 2:1). In 47BC he was made governor of Galilee, and in 40BC the Roman senate gave him the title 'King of the Jews', although he had to fight for his throne and his reign did not properly begin until 37BC. Highly regarded by the Romans, he was not popular with his Jewish subjects. Moreover, he had ten wives, and towards the end of his reign there was some plotting among his sons over who would succeed him. He actually executed three of his sons for intriguing against him. (The Roman emperor Augustus once remarked that he would rather be Herod's dog – some versions of the story say 'pig' – than Herod's son!) It is hardly surprising, therefore, that when Herod heard from the Magi of a newborn 'King of the Jews', but was unable to find the child, he acted with murderous determination to remove this potential rival by killing all the boys in and around Bethlehem who were two years old and under (Matthew 2:16). Since Herod died in 4BC, Jesus must have been born before that year.

Out-herod Herod

This phrase refers to the character and behaviour of Herod the Great, especially as portrayed in the medieval religious dramas known as mystery plays, in which he was always played as a ranting tyrant. To out-Herod Herod is, therefore, to behave even more cruelly or despotically, or to rant and shout even more loudly and excessively, than Herod. The phrase was used by William Shakespeare in *Hamlet*, where Hamlet is instructing some players not to overact when performing his play:

O! it offends me to the soul to hear a robustious periwig-pated fellow tear a passion to tatters, to very rags, to split the ears of the groundlings ... ...; it out-herods Herod: pray you, avoid it.

After the death of Herod the Great, his territory was divided between three of his sons: Archelaus became ruler of Judaea, Samaria and Idumaea (Matthew 2:22), Antipas was given Galilee and Peraea, and Philip was bequeathed the territories to the north-east of the Sea of Galilee. Brutal and tyrannical, Archelaus was deposed by the Romans in AD6. His territory then became a Roman province governed by officials appointed by the emperor. (Pontius Pilate was one such governor.)

ANTIPAS

Antipas was given the title 'Herod' when Archelaus was deposed. Herod Antipas is the Herod referred to as the tetrarch of Galilee in Luke 3:1. Antipas imprisoned John the Baptist for denouncing his marriage to Herodias, his half-brother Philip's wife (Matthew 14:3), marriage to a brother's wife being forbidden by the Jewish Law (Leviticus 20:21). It is Antipas that Jesus calls 'that fox' (Luke 13:31–32), and it is to Antipas, as ruler of Galilee, that Pilate sends Jesus when he discovers he is a Galilean (Luke 23:7). Antipas was deposed by the Romans in AD39.

Tetrarch

In the Roman empire, a tetrarch (from Greek *tetra* 'four' and *arche* 'rule') was the ruler of a quarter of a province or country.

THE TWO PHILIPS

Herod the Great had two sons named Philip. Both are mentioned in the Gospels (confusingly, in the same chapter!). Antipas' half-brother Philip became tetrarch of territory to the north-east of the Sea of Galilee after his father's death (Luke 3:1). He married his great-niece Salome, Herodias' daughter. He died in AD34. The other Philip was Herod Philip, whose wife Herodias left him for his half-brother Herod Antipas (Luke 3:19).

THE TWO AGRIPPAS

There are also two Agrippas mentioned in the New Testament. Herod Agrippa I is the 'Herod the king' of Acts 12:1. He was a grandson of Herod the Great. He was king first of the north-eastern territories, then also of Galilee and Peraea, and finally also of Judaea and Samaria. He died in AD44, struck down by the angel of the Lord for impiety (Acts 12:23).

> *Herodias was the sister of Herod Agrippa I. She first married Herod Philip, and then Herod Antipas. Both men were her uncles. She brought about the execution of John the Baptist through her daughter Salome. Salome married her great-uncle Philip (the tetrarch).*

Herod Agrippa II was the son of Herod Agrippa I. It is he who accused the apostle Paul of trying to make him a Christian (Acts 26:27–29). His sister Drusilla married the Roman governor Felix (Acts 24:24). Another sister, Bernice, accompanied Agrippa to hear Paul (Acts 25:13).

KEY TEACHINGS OF JESUS

THE BEATITUDES

The Beatitudes (Matthew 5:3–11) are part of what is known as the Sermon on the Mount:

Blessed are the poor in spirit: for theirs is the kingdom of heaven.

Blessed are they that mourn: for they shall be comforted.

Blessed are the meek: for they shall inherit the earth.

Blessed are they which do hunger and thirst after righteousness: for they shall be filled.

Blessed are the merciful: for they shall obtain mercy.

Blessed are the pure in heart: for they shall see God.

Blessed are the peacemakers: for they shall be called the children of God.

Blessed are they which are persecuted for righteousness' sake: for theirs is the kingdom of heaven.

Blessed are ye, when men shall revile you, and persecute you, and shall say all manner of evil against you falsely, for my sake.

✦ The word 'beatitude' means 'great blessedness'. It comes from Latin *beatus*, meaning 'happy, blessed'.

✦ The Sermon on the Mount is said to have taken place on the 'Horns of Hattin', a mountain in Galilee.

THE LORD'S PRAYER

Our Father which art in heaven, Hallowed be thy name. Thy kingdom come. Thy will be done in earth, as it is in heaven. Give us this day our daily bread. And forgive us our debts, as we forgive our debtors. And lead us not into temptation, but deliver us from evil: For thine is the kingdom, and the power, and the glory, for ever. Amen.
(Matthew 6:9–13)

✦ Luke's version of the prayer (11:2–4)

omits the last sentence.

✦ The word 'trespasses' comes in Jesus' comments on the prayer (Matthew 9:14–15):

For if ye forgive men their trespasses, your heavenly Father will also forgive you: But if ye forgive not men their trespasses, neither will your Father forgive your trespasses.

Luke's version of the prayer speaks of 'sins'.

The Two Great Commandments

A lawyer asked Jesus: Master, which is the great commandment in the law?
'Jesus said unto him, Thou shalt love the Lord thy God with all thy heart, and
with all thy soul, and with all thy mind. This is the first and great commandment.
And the second is like unto it, Thou shalt love thy neighbour as thyself. On these
two commandments hang all the law and the prophets.' (Matthew 22:36–40)

The first of these commandments is found in Deuteronomy (6:5) and the second in Leviticus (19:18).

The Golden Rule: Do unto others ...

Therefore all things whatsoever ye would that men should do to you, do ye
even so to them: for this is the law and the prophets. (Matthew 7:12)

When Rabbi Hillel, a famous Jewish teacher in the 1st centuries BC and AD, was asked to explain the Jewish Law in its shortest possible form, he replied: 'What you consider hateful, do not do to other people. That is the whole Law; the rest is just commentary.'

Jesus' mission

The Son of man is come to seek and to save that which was lost. (Luke 19:10)
I am come that they might have life, and that they might have it
more abundantly. (John 10:10)
The good shepherd giveth his life for the sheep. (John 10:11)

THE PARABLES OF JESUS

There are 25 parables in Matthew's gospel, nine in Mark, and 30 in Luke. Some parables are found in all three gospels, some in two, and some in only one of the three. (Of Luke's 30 parables, for example, 18 are found only in his gospel.) In total, there are 44 parables. There are no parables in John's gospel.

TEN WELL-KNOWN PARABLES

❶ THE GOOD SAMARITAN

A Samaritan helps an injured Jewish man when both a priest and a Levite (a temple assistant) have just walked past, and pays for him to be looked after while he recovers. This shows that he is the good neighbour.

Who were the Samaritans?

Samaritans are a religious group with beliefs similar to those of the Jews, but accepting only the five Books of Moses as Scripture. Their chief town was Shechem, close to present-day Nablus, and there was a temple on nearby Mount Gerizim. At the time of Jesus, there was great hostility between Jews and Samaritans. There are fewer than 1,000 Samaritans today.

❷ THE LOST SHEEP

If a man has 100 sheep, and one of them becomes lost, the man will go out and look for the lost sheep; and when he finds it, he will celebrate. In the same way, there will be celebrations in heaven when a sinner repents.

❸ THE PRODIGAL SON

A young man asks his father for the money he is due to inherit, and goes off and spends it on riotous living. Reduced to penury, he decides to risk going back home, ready to ask his father's forgiveness and become his servant. When the young man arrives, his father throws a party for him, so glad is he to see him safely home again. God too will welcome back a repentant sinner.

❹ THE RICH MAN AND LAZARUS

Lazarus is a poor man, reduced to eating bits of food that fall off a rich man's table. The two men die: Lazarus goes to heaven, the rich man to hell. He asks Abraham to send Lazarus back to warn his brothers so that they will not end up in hell too. Abraham says that they have had Moses and the prophets to warn them, and even if someone came back from the dead, that would not be enough to convince them.

The rich man is sometimes called 'Dives', which is simply the Latin word for 'rich'. In some ancient traditions he is given names such as Finaeus (= Phineas), Neves (or Nineves), Amonofis or Tantalus. Lazarus is not the same person as the man Jesus raised from the dead (John 11).

❺ THE PEARL OF GREAT PRICE

When a merchant found a valuable pearl, he sold everything he had in order to buy it. The kingdom of heaven is as valuable as that.

❻ THE WISE AND FOOLISH VIRGINS

Getting ready to meet a bridegroom, ten young women go out with their lamps. Five are wise and take plenty of oil with them, while five are foolish and don't take any spare oil. When the bridegroom finally arrives, the five who have no spare oil have to go off to buy some. When they return, they are not allowed in to the wedding feast. 'Watch therefore, for ye know neither the day nor the hour wherein the Son of man cometh.' (Matthew 25:13)

❼ THE TALENTS

A man gives his three servants five talents, two talents and one talent according to their ability. The first two double their money, which they give back to their master, while

the third simply buries his. The master is displeased by this and takes the talent away from him and gives it to the man with five talents. We should use our talents wisely whatever our circumstances.

A talent was both a weight and a large sum of money. It's from this story that 'talent' has taken the sense of 'aptitude' or 'skill'.

❽ THE SOWER AND THE SEED

A man sows corn on a field. Some of it is eaten by birds, some of it fails to take root, some of it grows but is choked by weeds, and only some of it produces more corn. This is like what happens to God's message in the world.

❾ SHEEP AND GOATS

When the Son of Man returns to judge the world, he will separate the righteous from the unrighteous, just like a shepherd separates the sheep from the goats.

❿ THE TWO BUILDERS

The wise man built his house on rock, whereas the foolish man built his house on sand. Similarly, a wise person takes Jesus' words as the foundation for their life, and acts on them.

'It is easier for a camel to go through the eye of a needle, than for a rich man to enter into the kingdom of God' (Matthew 19:24). A camel is a very large animal and the eye of a needle is a very small opening. There is no evidence that Jesus was talking about camels loaded with riches going through a narrow city gate, as is sometimes suggested. The Talmud (see page 63) talks about an elephant passing through the eye of a needle as something impossible.

THE 'I AM' SAYINGS OF JESUS

✳ *I am the bread of life.* (John 6:35)

✳ *I am the living bread which came down from heaven: if any man eat of this bread, he shall live for ever: and the bread that I will give is my flesh, which I will give for the life of the world.* (6:51)

✳ *I am the light of the world: he that followeth me shall not walk in darkness, but shall have the light of life.* (8:12)

✳ *I am the door of the sheep.* (10:7)

✳ *I am the door: by me if any man enter in, he shall be saved, and shall go in and out, and find pasture.* (10:9)

✳ *I am the good shepherd: the good shepherd giveth his life for the sheep.* (10:11)

✳ *I am the good shepherd, and know my sheep, and am known of mine.* (10:14)

✳ *I am the resurrection, and the life: he that believeth in me, though he were dead, yet shall he live.* (11:25)

✳ *I am the way, the truth, and the life: no man cometh unto the Father, but by me.* (14:6)

✳ *I am the true vine, and my Father is the husbandman.* (15:1)

A man who was merely a man and said the sort of things Jesus said would not be a great moral teacher. He would either be a lunatic – on a level with the man who says he is a poached egg – or else he would be the Devil of Hell. You must make your choice. Either this man was, and is, the Son of God: or else a madman or something worse. C S Lewis

Pharisees and Sadducees

Pharisees and Sadducees were two Jewish groups with differing viewpoints. For example, the Pharisees believed in the resurrection of the dead, but the Sadducees did not. Pharisees were noted for their scrupulous observance of the Jewish purity laws. They accepted oral tradition as well as the written Law, whereas the Sadducees did not.

For verily I say unto you, Till heaven and earth pass, one jot or one tittle shall in no wise pass from the law, till all be fulfilled. (Matthew 5:18)

A jot is the smallest letter of the Hebrew alphabet. A tittle is a small stroke that forms part of some letters of the Hebrew alphabet, rather like the serifs at the top of the letters *b, d, h, k, l* of the Roman alphabet.

JESUS' MIRACLES

physically handicapped, people suffering from leprosy, an ear that had been cut off (Luke 22:51), people suffering from other illnesses, and those under the control of demons

* raising the dead to life: a widow's son, Jairus' daughter, Lazarus
* feeding the 5,000 and the 4,000
* calming a storm and walking on water
* causing a large catch of fish (Luke 5:6) and finding the Temple tax in a fish (Matthew 17:27)
* changing water into wine at the marriage at Cana (John 2)
* healing the deaf, the blind, the
* cursing a fig tree which then withers (Matthew 21:19)

OTHER EXAMPLES OF THE DEAD BEING BROUGHT BACK TO LIFE:

a widow's son (by Ezekiel; 1 Kings 17) ✦ *the Shunnamite's son (by Elisha; 2 Kings 4)* ✦ *a corpse (by touching Elisha's bones; 2 Kings 13)* ✦ *Dorcas (by Peter; Acts 9)* ✦ *Eutychus (by Paul; Acts 20)*

The entry into Jerusalem According to legend, donkeys have had a dark cross on their backs from the time that Jesus rode a donkey into Jerusalem (Matthew 21).

THE LAST SUPPER

The last meal shared by Jesus and his disciples before the Crucifixion:
And he took bread, and gave thanks, and brake it, and gave unto them, saying, This is my body which is given for you: this do in remembrance of me. Likewise also the cup after supper, saying, This cup is the new testament in my blood, which is shed for you. (Luke 22:19–20)

In 1 Corinthians 11:20, this celebratory meal in the early church is called the Lord's supper.

The Holy Grail

The cup that Jesus used came to be known as the Holy Grail. Many legends grew up around it. According to one, Joseph of Arimathea had the cup and in it collected some of Christ's blood at the Crucifixion, which he then brought to England, where it disappeared or was kept by a line of guardians. Another version has the Grail brought from heaven to a castle and guarded by knights. The legends of the Holy Grail became entwined with the stories of King Arthur and the Knights of the Round Table. For some, the Grail refers to Mary Magdalene who, it is claimed, married Jesus and had a child: the Old French *san graal* 'holy grail' is interpreted as *sang real* 'royal blood'.

PONTIUS PILATE, THE MAN WHO WASHED HIS HANDS OF JESUS

When the Romans deposed Herod the Great's son Archelaus, ruler of Judaea and Samaria, in AD6, his territory became a Roman province governed by officials (known as prefects or procurators) appointed by the emperor. The fifth of these was Pontius Pilate.

Pilate was appointed in AD26, and governed the province until AD36, when he was ordered back to Rome to stand trial for cruelty and oppression. Nothing more is known of him for certain, but he may have committed suicide on the orders of the Roman emperor Caligula in AD39.

Pilate is described by historians of the time as obstinate, inflexible, harsh, brutal, spiteful and merciless. He frequently antagonized his Jewish subjects, e.g. by bringing into Jerusalem military standards bearing images of the emperor, so offending against the Second Commandment (though, faced with determined opposition from the Jews, he removed the standards six days later). In Luke 13:1, Jesus is told of some Galileans 'whose blood Pilate had mingled with their sacrifices'. This was perhaps during a riot in Jerusalem caused by Pilate using money from the Temple to pay for the building of an aqueduct, and may have been the reason for the enmity between Pilate and Herod Antipas (Luke 23:12), as Galileans would have been Antipas' subjects. Pilate's acquiescing to the Jewish authorities' demand that Jesus be crucified is seen by some as weak-willed and unprincipled, since he says clearly (Luke 23:14–15) that he can see no reason to execute Jesus, or as an act of cowardice in the face of Jewish threats to denounce him to the emperor (John 19:12), but it could perhaps be seen as merely pragmatic, to avoid yet another Jewish riot (Matthew 27:24).

WASH ONE'S HANDS

In Matthew 27:24, Pilate 'took water, and washed his hands before the multitude, saying, I am innocent of the blood of this just person'. This has given rise to the phrase 'to wash one's hands' of something, meaning to accept no responsibility for it:

The government washed their hands of the dispute, saying it was the responsibility of the local council.

In some later traditions, both Pilate and his wife (mentioned but unnamed in Matthew 27:19) were said to have become Christians. They have even been canonized as saints, Pilate in the Ethiopian Orthodox Church and his wife Procla (or Procula) in the Eastern Orthodox Church.

SAINTS' DAYS: *In the Ethiopian Church, the feast day of St Pontius Pilate and his wife is 25 June. In the Eastern Orthodox Church, St Procla's feast day is 27 October.*

PROCLA

Procla is sometimes called Claudia (or Claudia Procula or Claudia Procles, as for example in Mel Gibson's film *The Passion of the Christ*), and also Perpetua. Some ancient traditions make her the daughter of Julia, who was the daughter of the Roman emperor Augustus and wife of the emperor Tiberius, but there is no certain historical basis for this.

FELIX AND FESTUS

Pilate is not the only Roman procurator to be mentioned in the Bible. Antonius Felix was procurator from AD52 to 59 (Acts 23:24), and Porcius Festus from AD59 to 62 (Acts 24:27). Felix was the husband of Drusilla, the sister of Herod Agrippa II (Acts 24:24).

THE CRUCIFIXION

The place where Jesus was crucified was called Golgotha, which means 'place of a skull' (Matthew 27:33; Aramaic *gulgolta* 'skull'). 'Calvary' comes from the Latin equivalent: *Calvaria*, 'skull'.

STATIONS OF THE CROSS

The Stations of the Cross are a series of pictures or sculptures that depict incidents between Jesus' trial and burial. They are 14 in number:

Jesus is condemned to death ✞ The cross is laid on him ✞ His first fall ✞ He meets his mother ✞ Simon of Cyrene is made to carry the cross ✞ Jesus' face is wiped by Veronica ✞ His second fall ✞ He meets the women of Jerusalem ✞ His third fall ✞ He is stripped of his clothes ✞ He is crucified ✞ His death on the cross ✞ His body is taken down from the cross ✞ He is laid in the tomb.

♦ There may be a fifteenth station, depicting the Resurrection.

♦ The Stations of the Cross are also called the Way of the Cross (Latin *Via Crucis*) and the Way of Sorrows (Latin *Via Dolorosa*).

♦ According to legend, when St Veronica wiped Jesus' face, the image of his face was preserved on the cloth. A cloth many believe to be Veronica's is preserved in St Peter's Basilica in Rome.

♦ Although most depictions of the scene represent Jesus or Simon carrying the whole cross, it was probably only the cross-beam that they had to carry, that being the normal Roman practice in crucifixions.

♦ There is a legend that a robin picked a thorn out of the crown of thorns the soldiers had placed on Jesus' head. The blood issuing from the wound stained the robin's breast red.

JESUS' SEVEN WORDS FROM THE CROSS

The gospels record seven things Jesus said from the Cross, though no gospel records all seven. These are known as the 'seven words'.

Father, forgive them; for they know not what they do. (Luke 23:34)

✞

(To the thief) Verily I say unto thee, Today shalt thou be with me in paradise. (Luke 23:43)

✞

(To his mother) Woman, behold thy son! (To the disciple he loved) Behold thy mother! (John 19:26–27)

✞

My God, my God, why hast thou forsaken me? (Matthew 27:46)

✞

I thirst. (John 19:28)

✞

It is finished. (John 19:30)

✞

Father, into thy hands I commend my spirit. (Luke 23:46)

I.N.R.I

The letters I.N.R.I., sometimes seen on representations of the Crucifixion, stand for the Latin phrase *Iesus Nazarenus, Rex Iudaeorum* 'Jesus of Nazareth, the King of the Jews'. These were the words Pilate had written on a board placed on the cross above Jesus' head (John 19:19).

St Dysmas

One tradition has it that the 'good thief' crucified with Jesus, to whom Jesus promised paradise, was called Dysmas. The name of the other thief was Gestas. According to a myth well known in the Middle Ages, Dysmas and Gestas had actually tried to rob Joseph and Mary on their journey into Egypt (Matthew 1:14). However, Dysmas had paid Gestas to leave them alone. The infant Jesus had then predicted that the two men would be crucified with him, and that Dysmas would accompany him to paradise. The feast day of St Dysmas is 25 March.

In other legends, the two thieves are called Zoatham and Camma, or Joathas and Maggatras.

Invention of the Cross

'Invention' in this case means 'discovery'. There is a tradition that St Helena, the mother of the Roman emperor Constantine, made a trip to the Holy Land, and there searched for and found the cross on which Jesus was crucified.

STIGMATA

Stigmata are believed by many to be wounds, corresponding to the wounds Jesus received at the Crucifixion – nail wounds in his hands and feet, the wound from the spear thrust into his side on the cross, and head wounds from the crown of thorns – that appear on the bodies of certain people. Among the saints who have shown stigmata are:

St Francis of Assisi (the first person known to have received them)
• St Catherine of Siena • St Catherine of Genoa • St John of God
• St Catherine de' Ricci • St Mary Frances of the Five Wounds
• St Pio of Pietrelcina (Padre Pio)

The Turin Shroud

The Turin Shroud is a piece of linen cloth, about 14½ feet by 3½ (4.5m × 1 m) that bears the image of a man who appears to have been crucified. It is kept in the Cathedral of Saint John the Baptist in Turin, Italy. Many believe it to be the shroud in which Jesus' body was wrapped for burial.

THE RESURRECTION

In the end of the sabbath, as it began to dawn toward the first day of the week, came Mary Magdalene and the other Mary to see the sepulchre. And, behold, there was a great earthquake: for the angel of the Lord descended from heaven, and came and rolled back the stone from the door, and sat upon it. His countenance was like lightning, and his raiment white as snow: And for fear of him the keepers did shake, and became as dead men.

And the angel answered and said unto the women, Fear not ye: for I know that ye seek Jesus, which was crucified. He is not here: for he is risen, as he said. Come, see the place where the Lord lay. And go quickly, and tell his disciples that he is risen from the dead; and, behold, he goeth before you into Galilee; there shall ye see him: lo, I have told you. And they departed quickly from the sepulchre with fear and great joy; and did run to bring his disciples word. (Matthew 28: 1–8)

Matthew's gospel is the only one of the four to mention an earthquake. According to Luke's gospel (24:12):

> *Then arose Peter, and ran unto the sepulchre; and stooping down, he beheld the linen clothes laid by themselves, and departed, wondering in himself at that which was come to pass.*

JESUS' APPEARANCES AFTER THE RESURRECTION

The Prince of life, whom God hath raised from the dead; whereof we are witnesses (Acts 3:15)

After the resurrection Jesus appeared to:
Mary Magdalene and 'the other Mary' (Matthew 28:9) ❖ *the disciples (Matthew 28:17; Luke 24: 36–49; three occasions in John 20; 'many times' – Acts 1:3)* ❖ *two disciples on the way to Emmaus (Luke 24:13–35)* ❖ *more than 500 disciples (1 Corinthians 15:5)* ❖ *James (1 Corinthians 15:7)* ❖ *Paul (1 Corinthians 15:7)*

The Great Commission

And Jesus came and spake unto them, saying, All power is given unto me in heaven and in earth. Go ye therefore, and teach all nations, baptizing them in the name of the Father, and of the Son, and of the Holy Ghost: Teaching them to observe all things whatsoever I have commanded you: and, lo, I am with you alway, even unto the end of the world. (Matthew 28:18–20)

THE EARLY CHURCH

The story of the early church is told in the Acts of the Apostles, written by Luke as a continuation of his gospel story. Luke wrote the two books for Theophilus, about whom nothing is known for certain, though he may have been a Roman official.

The growth of the church

Numbers about 120 (Acts 1:15) ❖ 3,000 added (Acts 2:41) ❖ grows to 5,000 men (not counting women in this case; Acts 4:4) ❖ the number of disciples keeps growing (Acts 6:1) ❖ many thousands of Jews believe (Acts 21:20)

First martyr: Stephen (Acts 7) ❖ **First non-Jewish convert:** Cornelius (Acts 10) ❖ **First use of the word 'Christian':** in Antioch (Acts 11:26)

PAUL

FACTFILE

Original name: SAUL	*Conversion:* BY A VISION OF
Tribe: BENJAMIN	JESUS ON THE ROAD TO
Home city: TARSUS	DAMASCUS
Religious group: PHARISEES	*Death:* MARTYRED IN ROME
Occupation: TENTMAKER	

PAUL'S LETTERS

A likely order in which Paul's letters were written (though most of the dates are uncertain and disputed):

GALATIANS (C.48–49, BUT POSSIBLY C.52) ✠ 1 & 2 THESSALONIANS (C.51) ✠ 1 & 2 CORINTHIANS (C.53–55) ✠ PHILEMON (C.55 OR C.62) ✠ ROMANS (C.57–59) ✠ COLOSSIANS (C.60) ✠ EPHESIANS (C.60–61) ✠ PHILIPPIANS (C.57–59 OR C.61) ✠ 1 TIMOTHY, TITUS (C.63–65) ✠ 2 TIMOTHY (C.64–67)

PAUL'S TEACHING

If Christ be not risen, then is our preaching vain, and your faith is also vain. (1 Corinthians 15:14)

✳

All have sinned, and come short of the glory of God. (Romans 3:23)

✳

Justified freely by his grace through the redemption that is in Christ Jesus (Romans 3:24)

✳

The works of the flesh are manifest, which are these; adultery, fornication, uncleanness, lasciviousness, idolatry, witchcraft, hatred, variance, emulations, wrath, strife, seditions, heresies, envyings, murders, drunkenness, revellings, and such like. (Galatians 5:19–21)

✳

The fruit of the Spirit is love, joy, peace, longsuffering, gentleness, goodness, faith, meekness, temperance. (Galatians 5:22–23)

✳

Though I speak with the tongues of men and of angels, and have not charity, I am become as sounding brass, or a tinkling cymbal. And though I have the gift of prophecy, and understand all mysteries, and all knowledge; and though I have all faith, so that I could remove mountains, and have not charity, I am nothing. And though I bestow all my goods to feed the poor, and though I give my body to be burned, and have not charity, it profiteth me nothing.

Charity suffereth long, and is kind; charity envieth not; charity vaunteth not itself, is not puffed up, doth not behave itself unseemly, seeketh not her own, is not easily provoked, thinketh no evil; rejoiceth not in iniquity, but rejoiceth in the truth; beareth all things, believeth all things, hopeth all things, endureth all things.

Charity never faileth: but whether there be prophecies, they shall fail; whether there be tongues, they shall cease; whether there be knowledge, it shall vanish away. For we know in part, and we prophesy in part. But when that which is perfect is come, then that which is in part shall be done away. When I was a child, I spake as a child, I understood as a child, I thought as a child: but when I became a man, I put away childish things. For now we see through a glass, darkly; but then face to face: now I know in part; but then shall I know even as also I am known.

And now abideth faith, hope, charity, these three; but the greatest of these is charity. (1 Corinthians 13)

WHAT PAUL DID NOT SAY

*Paul did not say that money is the root of all evil. What he said was that
'the love of money is the root of all evil' (1 Timothy 6:10).*

Paul's missionary journeys

The first journey (AD46–48): Antioch (in Syria) – Seleucia (on the Mediterranean coast) – Cyprus (Salamis, Paphos) – (by sea north to) Perga – Antioch (in Pisidia, now Turkey) – Iconium – Lystra – Derbe – Antioch – Perga – Attalia – (by ship back to) Antioch in Syria.

The second journey (AD50–52): Antioch (in Syria) – Derbe – Lystra – Iconium – Troas (on what is now the coast of Turkey) – (by sea to the island of) Samothrace – (by sea to) Neapolis (in Macedonia) – Philippi – Amphipolis – Apollonia – Thessalonica – Berea – (south to) Athens and Corinth – Cenchrea – (by sea to) Ephesus (in western Turkey) – (by sea to) Jerusalem.

The third journey (AD53–57): Antioch (in Syria) – through Galatia and Phrygia (now modern Turkey) – Ephesus – through Macedonia and Greece – Philippi – (by sea to) Troas – Assos – (the island of) Mitylene – (the island of) Samos – Miletus – (the island of) Cos – (the island of) Rhodes – (by sea to) Patara – (by sea to) Tyre (on the coast of what is now Lebanon) – (south to) Ptolomais – Caesarea – Jerusalem.

ANTIOCH ❶ (Antioch in Pisidia) A town in what is now south-west Turkey. It sat on a major trading route; only ruins now remain. ❷ (Antioch in Syria) A city in southern Turkey, now Antakya, about 500 km (300 miles) north of Jerusalem. Paul and Barnabas spent a year there.

ATHENS A major city and centre of learning in Greece, now its capital. Visited by Paul, where he preached the gospel on the basis of an altar 'To the Unknown God'.

CAESAREA ❶ A city built by Herod the Great on the shore of the Mediterranean

Sea. Named in honour of the emperor Caesar Augustus. The official home of the Herod kings and the Roman governors.

2 (Caesarea Philippi) A town about 40 km (25 miles) north of the Sea of Galilee, also named in honour of Caesar Augustus, but with the addition of 'Philippi' (= of Philip the Tetrarch) to distinguish it from the other Caesarea.

COLOSSAE A town situated in what is now south-west Turkey. Paul's letters to the Colossians were written to the early church there. Philemon and his slave Onesimus were members of the church as Colossae.

CORINTH A town situated on the narrow neck of land that lies between central and southern Greece. Paul spent 18 months there during the second of his missionary journeys.

EPHESUS An important ancient city on what is now the west coast of Turkey. Paul's preaching outraged the craftsmen whose livelihood depended on the sale of objects related to the cult of the goddess Diana.

GALATIA An ancient region in what is now central Turkey. It is not certain which churches are being addressed by Paul in his letter to the Galatians.

PHILIPPI An important city near the coast of Macedonia, now in eastern Greece. Named by Philip of Macedon, father of Alexander the Great.

Letters not written by Paul

Hebrews (anonymous) ♦ James ♦ 1 & 2 Peter ♦ 1, 2 & 3 John ♦ Jude

And every priest standeth daily ministering and offering oftentimes the same sacrifices, which can never take away sins: But this man, after he had offered one sacrifice for sins for ever, sat down on the right hand of God. (Hebrews 10:11–12)

What doth it profit, my brethren, though a man say he hath faith, and have not works? Can faith save him? If a brother or sister be naked, and destitute of daily food, and one of you say unto them, Depart in peace, be ye warmed and filled; notwithstanding ye give them not those things which are needful to the body; what doth it profit? Even so faith, if it hath not works, is dead, being alone. (James 2:14–17)

A NEW HEAVEN AND A NEW EARTH: THE REVELATION OF ST JOHN THE DIVINE

The Revelation of St John is sometimes known as the Apocalypse (from Greek *apokalyptein* 'to reveal'). Apocalypses describe in visions, dreams and symbols the future triumph of God over evil. The books of Daniel and Revelation are examples of apocalyptic literature, as are parts of Ezekiel, Isaiah, Joel and Zechariah.

Some scholars think that the John who wrote Revelation was not the apostle John who wrote the gospel and three letters.

THE SEVEN CHURCHES IN ASIA

Ephesus ◆ Smyrna ◆ Pergamos ◆ Thyatira ◆ Sardis ◆ Philadelphia ◆ Laodicea

'Asia' was at that time the region of what is now western Turkey.

Scholars are not agreed as to whether the 'angels' of the churches (1:20) are actually angels (the guardian angels of the churches) or men (the bishops of the churches).

THE FOUR HORSEMEN OF THE APOCALYPSE

The first three horsemen are mounted, respectively, on a white horse, a red horse and a black horse. The fourth horseman, Death, rides a pale horse, and is closely followed by Hell. These four horsemen are agents of destruction:

◆ *The first horseman has a bow and was given a crown 'and he went forth conquering, and to conquer' (6:2).*

◆ *The second horseman is given a large sword 'and power to take peace from the earth' (6:4).*

◆ *The third horseman is holding a pair of scales (6:5).*

◆ *Death and Hell are given power 'over the fourth part of the earth, to kill with sword, and with hunger, and with death, and with the beasts of the earth' (6:8).*

The 'Four Horsemen of the Apocalypse' are traditionally named Conquest, War, Famine or Pestilence, and Death (or Death, War, Famine and Pestilence, or similar sets of names). Only Death is named as such in the Bible.

The 144,000

And I heard the number of them which were sealed: and there were sealed an hundred and forty and four thousand of all the tribes of the children of Israel. (7:4)

The number 12 being a symbol of completeness in the Bible, 12 times 12,000 also indicates completeness: not one of the elect will be lost.

666

'Let him that hath understanding count the number of the beast: for it is the number of a man; and his number is Six hundred threescore and six.' (13:18)

The 'man' is believed by many to be the Roman emperor Nero. Using gematria (see page 27), the consonant letters of Nero's name in Greek, when converted to Hebrew letters (*qsr nrwn*), add up to 666.

Some ancient manuscripts of the Bible have 616 instead of 666. This may come from dropping the final *n* or from using Greek letters and their values in the gematria rather than Hebrew letters.

Many other people have been suggested as candidates for the 666 label. Among these are:

☠ MARTIN LUTHER AND THE POPE ☠ NAPOLEON BONAPARTE, STALIN, HITLER AND SADDAM HUSSEIN ☠ the UNITED STATES OR ITS PRESIDENTS (SUCH AS RONALD REAGAN AND JOHN F KENNEDY) ☠ BILL GATES AND THE WORLD WIDE WEB

While some suggestions are perhaps not meant to be taken too seriously, some are intended to be absolutely serious. But given determination and ingenuity, you can probably point the 666 finger at almost anyone.

HOW IT ALL ENDS ... AND BEGINS AGAIN

John's visions end with the defeat of Satan, the judgement of the dead, a new heaven and a new earth, a new Jerusalem, and the return of Jesus.

Armageddon will be the site of the final battle between the forces of good and evil (16:16). *Har Megiddo* in Hebrew means 'the mountain of Megiddo'. Megiddo was the site of a number of battles in ancient times (see e.g. 2 Kings 23:29–30).